BUYING, OWNING, AND SELLING RHODE ISLAND WATERFRONT AND WATER VIEW PROPERTY

THE DEFINITIVE GUIDE TO PROTECTING YOUR PROPERTY RIGHTS AND YOUR INVESTMENT IN COASTAL PROPERTY

John M. Boehnert

Author of *Zoning the Oceans: The Next Big Step in Coastal Zone Management*

Buying, Owning, and Selling Rhode Island Waterfront and Water View Property

THE DEFINITIVE GUIDE TO PROTECTING YOUR PROPERTY RIGHTS AND YOUR INVESTMENT IN COASTAL PROPERTY

MR. & MRS. PRIMIS

I HOPE YOU WILL FIND THIS BOOK OF BENEFIT, GIVEN YOUR INTEREST IN RHODE ISLAND COASTAL PROPERTY.

ALL BEST!

John M. Boehnert

Greenwich Cove Press
An imprint of
Terra Firma LTD

terrafirma ltd

Disclaimer

The material in this book represents the individual author's own views and opinions and not the views and opinions of anyone else, including without limitation, the publisher, unless otherwise expressly stated herein.
Information set forth in this book is for general use and is not legal advice. Nothing contained in this book is to be considered the rendering of legal advice for specific cases, and readers are responsible for obtaining such advice from their own legal counsel. Given the fact-specific nature of legal questions, issues, and problems, reliance on a general discussion in this book to other specific factual situations is inappropriate and unwarranted. This book is intended for educational and informational purposes only. The offering of this book and its purchase is not intended to create, and does not constitute, an attorney-client relationship with the author or his law firm, and no such attorney-client relationship shall arise absent an engagement letter being entered into with the Law Offices of John M. Boehnert Ltd.

ISBN: 0692568964
ISBN 13: 9780692568965
Library of Congress Control Number: 2015957170
Greenwich Cove Press, East Greenwich, RI

To Matt and Kate,
quite literally, the joy of my life

CONTENTS

Acknowledgments

I am grateful to a number of people who helped me with various matters pertaining to this book.

Alexandra Graskemper, a very talented lawyer and an engaging personality, provided extensive research assistance and insights during the writing of this book, for which I am particularly grateful. I look forward to continued reports of her success in the practice of law. Krystin Alex also graciously provided research assistance in the early days of this book, for which I am grateful.

I very much appreciate then-Roger Williams University Law School Professor Susan Farady's guidance in seeking research assistance.

James Belliveau, one of the top title attorneys in Rhode Island, provided insight and guidance on a number of questions I raised during the writing of this book, and I very much appreciate his characteristic generosity.

Rhode Island Assistant Attorney General Michael Rubin, the state's long-time Environmental Advocate, was ever gracious and helpful in providing information to me on one of the significant waterfront property rights cases he was litigating as this book was being written.

I am also grateful for the assistance of a number of real estate professionals who gave their time to thoughtfully consider questions raised and provide information requested.

Peter Scotti, a well-known Rhode Island appraiser, was helpful to me in addressing some of the valuation issues pertaining to waterfront and water view property, and William Coyle III, another well-known Rhode Island real estate appraiser, was helpful to me in considering and addressing real estate property tax appeal questions. Similarly, James Ryan, an attorney experienced in real estate property tax valuation challenges, provided important background and insight on legal aspects of the tax appeal process. Richard Lipsitz, of Waterman Engineering Company, drew on his extensive background surveying properties abutting the ocean, rivers, and streams to provide significant insight on waterfront surveying issues.

The flood insurance program has been in flux nationally, as well as here in Rhode Island, and I very much appreciate the information and guidance provided by Grover Fugate, the veteran executive director of the Rhode Island Coastal Resources Management Council, as well as his "inside baseball" understanding of the inner workings of the flood insurance program. Also, insurance agent Matthew Amaral, who follows flood insurance issues closely, provided commentary on that portion of the book addressing flood insurance, and I very much appreciate the time he took to do so.

I also very much appreciate the always knowledgeable help of my administrative assistant, Remily Vaslet, who solves all problems cheerfully and, it seems, effortlessly.

I particularly want to thank my son, Matt, daughter, Kate, son-in-law Chris, and daughter-in-law, Amy, who provided hours of assistance, often at some pretty odd hours, as I raised questions or sought advice. I am tremendously grateful for their help, particularly in this age of caller ID on cell phones! Additionally, Kate, an experienced editor, also provided expert editorial assistance, greatly improving the original manuscript.

Over the years, I have also benefited greatly from interacting with some of Rhode Island's finest attorneys, who I think of as "old pros," although some are my age (which is certainly not old!) and some are younger. Many times these attorneys have been on the other side of the table, representing adverse parties. I am always pleased to see them involved in a transaction, whether we are working together or are adverse, as they greatly improve the results of the transaction, which is good for everyone. I have learned a great deal from these interactions, and some of that information is set forth in this book.

Finally, I want to extend my gratitude to so many clients over the years who have entrusted me with their matters and allowed me to assist them. To paraphrase Oliver Wendell Holmes Jr, the life of the law is not logic, it is experience. Without the years of experience I acquired from clients allow-ing me to represent their interests, I could not have written this book, for the most valuable information here is not "black letter law," but the judg-ment acquired from years of experience. And for that, I am truly grateful.

INTRODUCTION

The Purpose of This Book

The purpose of this book is to assist those buying, owning, and selling coastal property in Rhode Island in protecting their invest-ment and their property rights in what will likely be a significant financial transaction. While that is a narrow focus for a book, over thirty years of legal practice in Rhode Island in the areas of real estate, land use, environmental law, and coastal permitting have convinced me that such a book is necessary. Indeed, some of the carnage I have seen over the years arising from buyers and owners not protecting themselves has been heartbreaking.

The Problem

Examples include the couple who bought coastal property to build their second home and ultimate retirement haven, only to have a necessary environmental permit revoked by the same agency that issued it. This resulted in a nearly twenty-year battle, including expensive litigation, be-fore my firm (which came to the situation late) was able to get permits for construction, and even that required more litigation.

Another case, in which I was not personally involved, saw a dentist buy waterfront property and attempt to build a vacation retreat for his family, including eight youngsters. He finally got the necessary permits, but it took fifteen years. As he said, "We feel we won, but they still beat us." By the time his vacation retreat was finally under construction, all his children had grown and left home.

I have seen waterfront property purchased without a survey only to find that part of the business being purchased was not located on the property purchased.

I have seen property owners find out years after owning waterfront property that a portion of the property between them and the beach was owned by the state, not them, and they therefore were no longer waterfront property owners (nor, for that matter, the owner of the land on which a part of their sewage disposal system was located).

I have seen contentious disputes between neighbors over access to waterfront property and disputes over water views.

I have seen a couple purchase waterfront property and subsequently initiate litigation to quiet title to the ownership of a portion of that waterfront property.

And in a case that I successfully took to the Rhode Island Supreme Court, I have seen the State claim title to hundreds of millions of dollars of filled tidal land (i.e., land created by the placement of fill below mean high tide), claiming the businesses, institutions, and utility companies that had "owned" the land for over a century were effectively trespassers. It was proposed that these property "owners" would need to pay a licensing fee to continue to use "their" property. In this case, the Rhode Island Supreme Court ruled in favor of the property owners, and we were able to clear title to those properties despite the State's claim.

As I have written in the past, waterfront property owners can be forgiven if they feel that war has been declared on them. Waterfront and water view property is highly regulated, and in Rhode Island, private property within the jurisdiction of the primary coastal regulator is severely restricted. For example, if your property is in a coastal buffer zone, the state can tell you that you will not cut the grass or vegetation without their approval, including even dead vegetation. Moreover, your view corridors to the water may be limited, and you may be required to secure governmental consent if you want to cut trees or shrubbery to expand your view of the water that you likely paid a great deal to be near. You may also be prevented from planting flowers or other nonindigenous plantings, and your ability to install a canoe or kayak rack or a picnic area may require consent from the government. And of course, any of those consents can be denied.

When people hear this, they are often stunned, but those are the regulations, and you violate them at your peril. And these are just some of the many regulations by one of several federal, state, and local regulators that govern coastal properties.

Moreover, members of the public often feel that they are entitled to traverse and even use private waterfront property, and private citizens and citizen groups, including environmental organizations, are often quite vocal and aggressive in seeking to monitor and restrict the development and use of coastal properties. Such groups often intervene in or appear before permitting proceedings to block relief sought by property owners. As I write this, at least one such group is actively opposing efforts by Rhode Island's primary coastal regulator to allow certain decisions to be made by staff as opposed to by the full council after hearing (a more time-consuming and expensive procedure) because they think staff review denies them full input into the decision-making process.

The simple fact is that coastal property in Rhode Island is highly desirable and highly regulated. Moreover, environmental groups as well as neighbors often seek to limit or restrict what can be done on coastal property under private ownership, often to the detriment of the private property owners, and disputes between and among coastal property owners are common—including disputes leading to litigation.

The Solution

Transactions involving coastal properties must be approached carefully by both buyers and sellers. In particular, this specifically includes appropriate due diligence investigations by buyers, the scope of which depends in part on the type of property being acquired, the reasons for the acquisition, and specific property characteristics.

Owners of coastal properties, particularly those building or expanding on coastal properties (whether residences, businesses, docks, or other in-water structures) must be vigilant to ensure that they are complying with all applicable federal, state, and local laws, rules, and regulations—some of which, incidentally, may conflict with one another. Furthermore, projects of any material scope may well require a team of experts, perhaps including lawyers, engineers, wetlands biologists, contractors, environmental scientists, surveyors, etc. And it should be a team carefully tailored to the particular project.

Buyers and owners must understand the regulatory environment that governs them and their property upon acquisition, they must understand what they can and cannot do, what their property rights are, and what limitations or restrictions may impact those property rights. Perhaps more importantly, they must understand how to navigate the regulatory process to get the consents, approvals, and permits that they need.

Sellers must know what they may need to do before putting their property on the market, how to address required disclosures, what issues they should consider in structuring their sale transaction, and what they should and should not do in negotiating a purchase and sale transaction.

This book addresses all those issues in detail.

The Approach

This book is segmented into three sections—one addressing issues primarily pertaining to buyers, the second addressing issues primarily pertaining to owners, and the final segment addressing issues primarily pertaining to sellers.

That being said, it is recommended that whether you are a prospective purchaser, a current owner, or a seller, you read the entire book. Successful buyers will in fact become owners, and eventually owners may become sellers. Sellers should understand the advice being given to buyers because perhaps their buyer may have read this book too!

Also, from a practical standpoint, the segment focused on current owners addresses development of raw land or improved property slated for redevelopment, and this will provide insights to a buyer that may impact his or her due diligence activities, contractual provisions, or pricing for the purchase itself.

While I have tried to get everything right here, it is perhaps inevitable that there will be some lapses where something has not been thoroughly explained, or some potentially useful information may have been omitted, or even where something has been misstated. To the extent I become aware of that, I will correct it promptly, and to the extent that readers would call my attention to any such matters, I would be grateful.

One final notation—while this book is admittedly narrowly focused, particular care has nevertheless been taken to ensure that it is tightly written in order to respect your time. I have taken seriously President Lincoln's admonishment to "take the time to be brief." Where further exploration may be appropriate for those seeking more detail, I have provided citations or suggested reading. However, because this book is intended for laymen, legal citations have been strictly limited. That being said, I suspect that many lawyers and real estate professionals who do not specialize in waterfront or water-view properties, including realtors and consultants, will find this book of significant value; at least, I certainly hope so!

PART 1

BUYING COASTAL PROPERTY

A lthough this section of the book provides a brief overview of the coastal areas available in Rhode Island, it is not intended to be a real estate guide. There are excellent realtors and real estate firms in Rhode Island that are more than qualified to perform those functions. Rather, while I provide a very brief schematic orientation to coastal properties in Rhode Island to assist those unfamiliar with Rhode Island in exploring the range of coastal opportunities, the primarily purpose of Part I is to help buyers understand the legal and regulatory issues they face in buying coastal property. Property acquisition is not just a financial transaction; it is a legal transaction as well. Coastal properties are not only some of the most highly regulated properties in Rhode Island, but they also often implicate legal issues that are not common to noncoastal properties.

Part I is designed to provide a buyer with useful information that he or she can reference in navigating his or her way through the legal and regulatory thicket, and, if he or she so desires, in acquiring a suitable coastal property.

CHAPTER 1

AN INTRODUCTION TO RHODE ISLAND COASTAL PROPERTIES

A s Rhode Island's official government website notes, Rhode Island is the smallest state in the union with the longest official name of any state (State of Rhode Island and Providence Plantations). This is in many ways a fitting introduction to a state of contrasts.

While it is the eighth least populous state, it is one of the most densely populated states, with 1,016 people per square mile, trailing only New Jersey. (The District of Columbia is more densely populated but is, of course, not a state.) Municipalities range from Providence, with its excellent restaurants, charming Ivy League campus, historic East Side, and increasingly flattering ratings from both tourists and residents alike, to Newport, with its spectacular mansions, colonial architecture, and remarkable boating and sailing venues, to tiny Central Falls, a former mill city of 19,400 people wedged into only 1.29 square miles, making it the most densely populated city in Rhode Island and the twenty-fourth most densely populated incorporated area in the country.

According to one historical theory, Rhode Island derives its name from "Roodt Eylandt," Dutch for "red island," bestowed by Dutch explorer Adrian Block either for the red clay found at its shores or for red autumnal foliage, depending on which version of this historical theory you accept. Another theory has the name originating with an earlier explorer who named a large island "Rhodes," after the Ottoman island so named. Not to further confuse things, but the official name for the island on which

Newport, Middletown, and Portsmouth are located is "Rhode Island." To avoid confusion, the island is generally referred to as Aquidneck Island.

In addition to their being several theories as to the origin of the state's name (Rogues Island is yet another one), Rhode Island also has several nicknames, including "Little Rhody," the "Plantation State," and the "Ocean State." The latter is perhaps the most popular, at least since it was put on the state license plate in 1972. It is an apt name.

The state measures approximately forty-eight miles long by thirty-seven miles wide and has a land area of 1,033.81 square miles according to the US Census Bureau, or 1,045 square miles according to Wikipedia. However, its total area is approximately 15 percent larger (or 1,214 square miles) by Rhode Island secretary of state records, given the extensive bays and inlets of the state, including Narragansett Bay.

Rhode Island borders the Atlantic Ocean, Rhode Island Sound, and Narragansett Bay, and has forty miles of coastline. Yet, when all inlet and tidal areas are included, the National Oceanic and Atmospheric Administration calculates the Rhode Island shoreline as 384 miles. A map of Narragansett Bay is included in Table 1A and a map of the southern Rhode Island coast is included in Table 1B. As can be seen on the maps, Narragansett Bay separates Rhode Island. The mainland communities are generally referred to as the West Bay, with Aquidneck Island (Newport, Middletown, and Portsmouth) and Jamestown in the center of the bay, and Barrington, Bristol, Warren, Tiverton, and Little Compton referred to as the East Bay.

In keeping with the moniker Ocean State, more than half of Rhode Island's cities and towns are coastal communities, and no Rhode Islander lives more than a thirty-minute drive from the shore—and of course, thousands live within a walk of the shore. The list of coastal communities in this book is the result of a little subjective judgment. Of the twenty municipalities I characterize as coastal communities, I have not included a city or town that may only have a comparatively modest presence on what may be a tidal river (and thus considered a coastal feature for purposes of coastal regulation), such as Central Falls or Pawtucket, but I have included Providence and East Providence, given their locations on significant tidal rivers. The listing of cities and towns, with some further identifying information, is included in Table 1C, along with a list of noncoastal cities and towns that includes references to some significant nontidal, noncoastal waterways in those municipalities for your interest and perhaps exploration.

These coastal areas include a broad mix of communities and coastal characteristics. They range from the quaint historic town of East Greenwich, with a very small coastline on Greenwich Cove, to Narragansett, with its extensive coastline and dramatic beaches where surfing is popular (and where Clams Casino was invented at the old waterfront Casino Restaurant). These communities include Charlestown, with not only a Block Island Sound coastline, but stunning ponds such as Ninigret Pond, a large saltwater pond or lagoon, and Jamestown, on Conanicut Island, the second largest island in Narragansett Bay and a short bridge crossing to Newport. For greater variety, there is Little Compton, a rural East Bay community with pastoral farmland and a coastline on the Sakonnet River and the Atlantic Ocean, where it is easy to feel that you have stepped back more than a century in time. And there is New Shoreham, a small town on Block Island, approximately twelve miles south of the Rhode Island mainland, a charming town that enjoys ocean beaches as well as the Great Salt Pond.

And speaking of ponds and islands, Rhode Island has them in abundance. Many of the ponds are in "South County" (a misnomer since there is technically no Rhode Island county by that name). The term refers to Washington County, which encompasses approximately the lower third of the Rhode Island mainland and includes the coastal communities of North Kingstown, South Kingstown, Charlestown, and Westerly as well as New Shoreham (Block Island). Most of these coastal ponds are saltwater, tidal, and spectacular recreation areas for fishing, boating, swimming, quahogging, nature walks, and just beaching. Some of the more popular ponds include the Great Salt Pond in New Shoreham, Quonochontaug Pond in Westerly and Charlestown, Ninigret Pond in Charlestown, Greenhill Pond in South Kingstown, Point Judith Pond in Charlestown and Narragansett, Winnapaug Pond in Westerly, and Potter Pond in South Kingstown. Some of these ponds are large enough to accommodate someone who wants to live on "the ocean" and many residences in these areas have views across the ponds to the ocean.

As for islands, it is little surprise that Rhode Island has them. Many of them are major, such as Aquidneck Island, which is the largest island in

Narragansett Bay and is home to Newport, Middletown, and Portsmouth. Conanicut Island is occupied by the town of Jamestown, which has a population of a little over five thousand residents and an increasing number of summer residents. Block Island, where the town of New Shoreham is located, has a little more than one thousand year round residents and substantially more in summer months. There are over thirty islands in Narragansett Bay, most of them not populated. The islands range from Aquidneck Island's 37.8 square miles to tiny Whale Rock, the smallest island in Narragansett Bay, situated in the west passage of the bay in Narragansett. Whale Rock was named for its whale back shape, and a lighthouse installed on it to warn ships and avoid shipwrecks was destroyed in the 1938 hurricane.

Many of the islands have colorful names, such as Rat Island, Goat Island, Fox Island, Rabbit Island, Hope Island, Rose Island, Dutch Island, Patience Island, and Prudence Island. And some of the smaller islands, like Prudence Island and Goat Island, are inhabited.

The important point to understand about Rhode Island coastal properties is that in a comparatively small area you have an extensive coastline and a suite of options for coastal investment. You can live in a quiet, remote, rural area with a great deal of charm and pastoral beauty, such as Little Compton, perhaps on a working farm if you so choose. You can live in a bustling urban environment within a short walk of restaurants, nightlife, and shopping, such as Newport. You can live on an island in a house you custom build on a waterfront or water-view lot. You can live in a beach community and walk to a beach. Or, like Taylor Swift, you can buy an iconic mansion in Watch Hill, Westerly, paying a rumored seventeen million dollars—a significant discount from the original twenty-four million dollar asking price.

The specifics of these opportunities I leave to realtors. My primary interest is in ensuring that whatever options and opportunities you select, you conduct proper due diligence and that you understand, and comply with, applicable laws, rules, and regulations.

Table 1A
Narragansett Bay

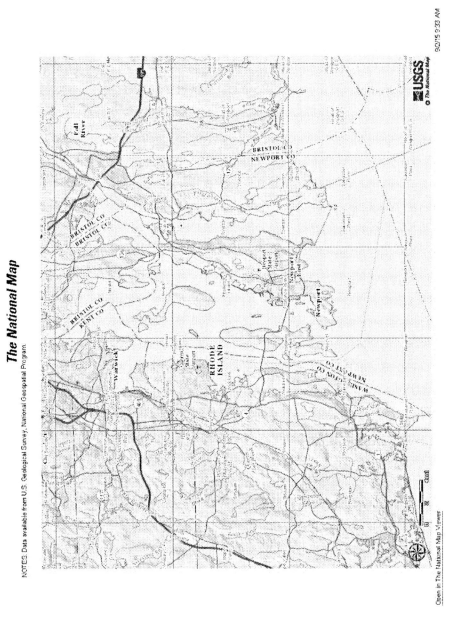

Table 1B
South Bay

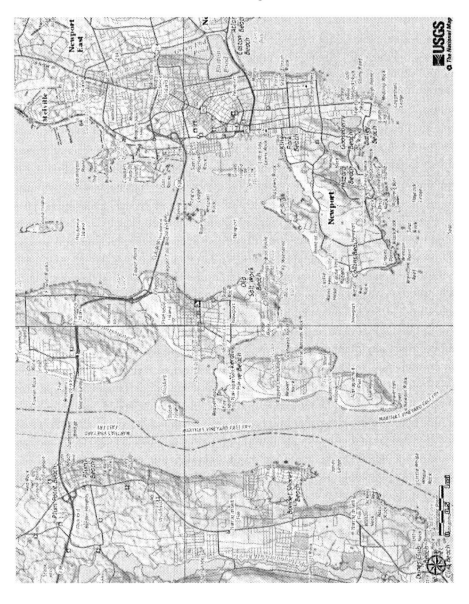

Table 1C
Coastal Cities and Towns

Barrington

- 8.4 square miles
- Borders Palmer River, Narragansett Bay, and Bullocks Cove
- Contains 100-acre cove, Barrington River through Tyler Point to Warren River, down to Adams Point, Brickyard Pond, and Echo Lake

Bristol

- 10.1 square miles
- Bordered by Mount Hope Bay and Narragansett Bay and home to a deepwater port

Charlestown

- 36.8 square miles
- On the coast of Block Island Sound
- Contains Watchaug Pond, Ninigret Pond

Cranston

- 28.6 square miles
- Mostly inland, with eastern boundary on Narragansett Bay

East Greenwich

- 16.6 square miles
- Mostly inland with exception of tract of land touching Greenwich Bay and Greenwich Cove

East Providence

- 13.4 square miles
- Western coast runs along the Seekonk River to Providence River into Narragansett Bay
- Omega Pond

Jamestown

- 9.7 square miles
- Sits in Narragansett Bay
- Contains Dutch Island Harbor, Mackerel Cove, Cranston Cove, Potter Cove, and Hull Cove

Little Compton

- 20.9 square miles
- Borders Sakonnet River and Atlantic Ocean
- Contains Simmons Pond, Long Pond, Tunipus Pond, Watson Reservoir, Round Pond, Briggs Marsh, and Quicksand Pond

Middletown

- 13 square miles
- Located on Aquidneck Island in Narragansett Bay
- Contains South Easton Pond, North Easton Pond, Gardiner Pond, and Nelson Paradise Pond

Narragansett

- 14.2 square miles
- Borders Narragansett Bay and the Pettaquamscutt River
- Contains Lake Conochet/Little Neck Pond, Sprague Pond, and Wesquage Pond

New Shoreham

- 9.7 square miles
- Located on Block Island and surrounded by the Atlantic Ocean
- Contains Fresh Pond, Sands Pond, Sachem Pond, Middle Pond, Clayhead Swamp Peckham Pond, Harbor Pond, Mill Tail Swamp and Pond, Trims Pond, Rodman Pond, and Motts Pond

Newport

- 7.9 square miles
- Located on Aquidneck Island and borders Narragansett Bay, Sakonnet River, Rhode Island Sound
- Contains Lily Pond, Almy Pond, South Easton Pond, and North Easton Pond (Green End Pond)

North Kingstown

- 43.6 miles
- Borders Narragansett Bay
- Contains Kettle Hole Pond, Silver Spring Lake, Secret Lake, Oak Hill Pond, Annaquatucket Mill Pond, Belleville Pond, Davol Pond, Frys Pond, Potowomut, and Carr Pond

Portsmouth

- 23.2 square miles
- Located on Aquidneck Island in Narragansett Bay
- Includes Prudence Island, Hog Island, Hope Island, and Patience Island
- Lawton Valley Reservoir, Saint Mary's Pond, Sisson Pond, and Melville Ponds

Providence

- 18.5 square miles
- Borders Providence Harbor
- Contains Mashapaug Pond and Roger Williams Park Ponds

South Kingstown

- 57.1 square miles
- Borders Block Island Sound
- Contains Green Hill Pond, Trustom Pond, Tucker Pond, Worden Pond, White Pond, Long Pond, Peddlers Pond, Hot House Pond, Round Pond, Wash Pond, Little Wash Pond, Potter Pond, Fresh Pond, Glen Rock Reservoir, Cedar Swamp Pond, Factory Pond, Mill Pond, Bull Head Pond, Peace Dale Reservoir, Indian Lake, Larkin Pond, Barber Pond, Yawgoo Pond, Asa Pond, Thirty Acre Pond, Saugatucket Pond, Silver Lake, and Hundred Acre Pond

Tiverton

- 29.4 square miles
- Borders Mount Hope Bay and eastern shore of Narragansett Bay
- Contains Stafford Pond, Nonquit Pond, and Creamer Pond

Warren

- 6.2 square miles
- Borders Warren River, Kickemuit River, Palmer River, and Mount Hope Bay

Warwick

- 35.5 square miles
- Borders Greenwich Bay and Narragansett Bay

- Contains Posnegansett Pond, Spring Green Pond, Warwick Pond, Gorton Pond, Sand Pond, Sandy Pond (Little Pond), and Three Ponds

Westerly

- 30.1 square miles
- Borders Pawcatuck River into Little Narragansett Bay, Block Island Sound
- Contains saltwater ponds such as Maschaug Pond, Winnapaug Pond, and Quonochontaug Pond, and a freshwater lake, Chapman Pond

Inland Cities and Towns

Burrillville

- 55.6 square miles
- Mostly inland
- Contains Spring Lake, Wilson Reservoir, and Sucker Pond
- Touches Wallum Lake and Slaterville Reservoirs

Central Falls

- 1.2 square miles
- Boarders Blackstone River

Coventry

- 59.5 square miles
- Contains Stump Pond, Flat River Reservoir, Quidnick Reservoir, Arnold Pond, Whitford Pond, Great Grass Pond, Reynolds Pond, Maple Root Pond, and Tiogue Pond

Cumberland

- 26.8 square miles

Exeter

- 57.7 square miles
- Touches Beach Pond

Foster

- 51.1 square miles
- Contains most of Barden Reservoir

Glocester

- 54.8 square miles
- Contains Ponaganset Reservoir and Smith and Sayles Reservoir

Hopkinton

- 43 square miles
- Contains Blue Pond, Yawgoog Pond, Wincheck Pond, and Locustville Pond

Johnston

- 23.7 square miles
- Contains Oak Swamp Reservoir, Almy Reservoir Simmons Upper reservoir, Simmons Lower Reservoir, and Kimball Reservoir

Lincoln

- 18.2 square miles
- Contains Handy Pond, Laporte's Pond, Oleny Pond, Wenscott Reservoir, Scott Pond, and Barney Pond

North Providence

- 5.7 square miles
- Contains Canada Pond and Wenscott Reservoir (Twin Rivers)

North Smithfield

- 24 square miles
- Contains Woonsocket Reservoir #1, Woonsocket Reservoir #2, Tarkiln Pond, Trout Brooke Pond, Lake Bel Air, Todd's Pond, Woonsocket Reservoir #3, Primrose Pond, and Slatersville Pond

Pawtucket

- 8.7 square miles
- Contain s Arnold Mills Reservoir (Pawtucket Reservoir), Slater Park Pond, and Blackstone River

Richmond

- 40.6 square miles
- Contains Frying Pan Pond, Canob Pond, Meadowbrook (Sandy Pond), Browning Mill Pond (Arcadia Pond), Carolina Trout Pond, White Brook Pond, and Grass Pond

Scituate

- 48.7 square miles
- Contains Regulating Reservoir, Moswanicut Pond, Scituate Reservoir, King Pond, Westconnaug Pond, Barden Reservoir, Brush Meadow Pond, Pine Swamp Pond, and Betty Pond

Smithfield

- 26.6 miles square miles
- Contains Upper Sprague Reservoir, Woonsocket Reservoir #3, Stillwater Pond, Harris Pond, Mountaindale Reservoir, Wenscott Reservoir (Twin Rivers), Georgiaville Pond, Hawkins Pond, Slack Reservoir, Waterman Reservoir, Woonasquatucket Reservoir, and Lower Sprague Reservoir

West Greenwich

- 50.6 square miles
- Contains Wickaboxet Pond, Carr Pond, Tippencansett Pond, Tillinghast Pond, Hazard Pond, Capwell Mill Pond, Phelps Pond, Great Grass Pond, Eisenhower Lake, Breakheart Pond, Mishnock Lake, Reynolds Pond, and Tarbox Pond

West Warwick

- 7.9 square miles
- Contains Matteson Pond

Woonsocket

- 7.7 square miles
- Blackstone River runs through
- Contains Social Pond

CHAPTER 2

THE REGULATORY ENVIRONMENT

Any introduction to the purchase of coastal property in Rhode Island should begin with an overview and understanding of the Rhode Island regulatory environment as it pertains to such property. As noted, waterfront and water-view property is heavily regulated in Rhode Island, often by regulators with overlapping jurisdiction, and sometimes by regulators imposing either contradictory regulations or regulations that raise questions as to what a property owner can or cannot do. And often this is by design. It is not uncommon for a proposed activity, such as construction of a house on a waterfront parcel, to require the approval of several municipal and state permitting agencies, and perhaps even federal regulators.

Cities and Towns

From a regulatory perspective we start with cities and towns, as there is no form of county government in Rhode Island. But first, a word about regulatory entities is appropriate. While one may think of regulators as agencies like the Environmental Protection Agency (which certainly is a regulator and a powerful one at that), cities and towns themselves are regulatory jurisdictions by virtue of their permitting and enforcement authority. The ability to issue permits generally entails the concomitant power to deny permits. And the ability to promulgate regulations generally involves the authority to enforce those regulations with fines or more punitive measures. It is the increasingly rare governmental entity today that is purely advisory without regulatory authority. And it is not uncommon to find that obscure boards such as a local historic district commission, with appointed members, have significant authority—including the ability to tell you that no, you will not put an addition on that colonial house, or to allow an addition but mandate that they, and not your architect, will tell you how it will look. I saw one case recently where a local historic board held up an addition to a home for several years until the homeowner finally gave up and settled for rehabbing only the interior of the home. When you see a government entity, no matter how small, if you think "regulator" you may be more often right than wrong.

In Rhode Island, municipalities derive their authority from the state, whether it is to tax real estate or control the zoning and subdivision of land. For example, a state enabling statute, the Rhode Island Zoning Enabling Act of 1991 (RI Gen. Laws 45–24–27 through 45–24–72), empowers and authorizes municipalities to adopt and enforce zoning ordinances consistent with the requirements of the zoning enabling act. Similarly, another Rhode Island statute, the Rhode Island Land Development and Subdivision Review Enabling Act of 1992 (RI Gen. Laws 45–23–25 through 45–23–77), empowers and authorizes municipalities to control the subdivision and development of land, whether for minor development projects such as the construction of a house or for large mixed use development. Without such state authority, municipalities would not have the power to so regulate.

Given this state authority, municipalities have extensive regulatory jurisdiction over coastal properties principally through their issuance of building permits and enforcement of the state building code and through their control of the subdivision approval and land development process. How this work is done can vary in some instances from community to community, with larger cities having greater staff resources than smaller towns. However, generally a building official and a zoning official enforce the building code and zoning ordinances, and a planning board addresses subdivisions and major and minor land development plans. A zoning board of review will address zoning deviations, variances, special exceptions, and alleged violations of the zoning ordinances. Zoning and building officials, who often have construction or engineering backgrounds, are generally full-time municipal employees, as is a municipal planner (although this may be a part-time position in smaller communities), while planning boards and zoning boards are often volunteer uncompensated appointees. These appointees are often highly knowledgeable about the subjects they review and render decisions upon, being architects, planners, builders, realtors, etc., but they are sometimes novices who are getting an education each time they attend a meeting.

Municipal regulation of coastal properties is discussed in more detail in chapter 4, dealing with due diligence in the acquisition of coastal properties. Additionally, chapter 7, addressing construction on coastal properties, addresses one issue with potentially significant impact on coastal property owners building or expanding structures—the increasing tendency of municipalities to enact regulations conflicting with state regulatory authorities and limiting or restricting improvement of coastal properties.

State Regulators

There are several state regulators of coastal properties. Although these regulators have varying degrees of jurisdiction and impact on such properties, ranging from minor to extreme, it is important to identify the primary players as the nature of a particular coastal property and its current or proposed use may make a minor state regulator very important for that particular property. This discussion will not be in order of importance; in fact, I will discuss last the most important Rhode Island coastal regulator, the Rhode Island Coastal Resources Management Council (CRMC). This organization considers itself the permitting agency of last resort for matters pertaining to coastal properties. In other words, it takes the position that before you come to the CRMC for a permit, known as an Assent, you must obtain permits from all other local, state, and federal agencies with permitting jurisdiction over the property in question. Accordingly, it will be discussed last in this discussion of state regulators.

The Rhode Island Department of Environmental Management

The Rhode Island Department of Environmental Management (RIDEM or DEM) is the primary environmental regulator in Rhode Island, enforcing state environmental laws and regulations pertaining to clean water, clean air, onsite sewage systems, and hazardous waste, among others.

While the Environmental Protection Agency (EPA) retains concurrent jurisdiction over the enforcement of federal statutes and regulations in Rhode Island and certainly does undertake enforcement activity in Rhode Island, the EPA delegates enforcement of many of these programs to the DEM when it is satisfied that the state statutes and regulations adequately regulate the area subject to federal regulation. Accordingly, the likelihood is that if a business person or developer encounters an environmental regulator under any of these federally delegated programs, that regulator will be from the DEM rather than the EPA.

DEM regulates a wide swatch of Rhode Island environmental activities, including air emissions, discharges to water bodies and ground water, hazardous waste disposal, oil pollution, individual sewage disposal systems, mercury regulations, dredging and management of dredge materials (in conjunction with the Coastal Resources Management Council), underground storage facilities for petroleum and hazardous materials, solid waste, onsite waste water treatment systems, wetlands, storm water regulation, and site remediation regulations.

The DEM's website contains current rules and regulations and references to statutes administered by the DEM. This website is found at www.dem.ri.gov/.

By way of example, a purchaser or owner of coastal property in Rhode Island could find himself dealing with the DEM pertaining to permits or violations for individual sewage disposal systems, hazardous waste, solid waste, wetlands (depending on proximity to the coast), underground storage tanks, site remediation, oil pollution, storm water regulation, dredging, or discharges to water bodies. That could be just for a residential purchaser. If the owner was an operating business, jurisdictional issues could include, in addition to the foregoing lists, such matters as mercury regulation or air emissions.

DEM has its own Administrative Adjudication Division with dedicated hearing officers who hear first level appeals from agency decisions. Those hearing officer decisions are subject to review by DEM's Director, as well as to court appeal under the Administrative Procedures Act.

The Department of Environmental Management is a regulator which cannot be ignored in Rhode Island.

The Rhode Island Department of Health

The Rhode Island Department of Health (DOH) is often overlooked as an environmental regulator, but it does have several environmental regulatory functions. First, it is the primary regulator for asbestos, and to the extent the existence or abatement of asbestos is at issue, the DOH will be involved. Removal of asbestos will require filing an asbestos abatement plan with the department and seeking its approval. With regard to coastal properties, this jurisdiction generally would not be implicated unless planned activity involved renovation of a historic structure or older industrial or business facilities.

The DOH also exercises regulatory authority with regard to lead poisoning and administers certain educational and training requirements for repairs and renovations involving lead-based paint, more specifically detailed on its website. Again, this jurisdiction likely would not be implicated regarding coastal properties unless planned activities involved rehabilitation of a historic structure or industrial or business facilities (note also the jurisdiction of the Housing Resources Commission as the lead state agency for lead hazard mitigation, which is also referenced on the DOH's website).

The DOH also regulates water supply wells, in addition to private and public water supply systems. For example, if a developer is considering permitting a development project or taking over a development project during build out, which will utilize an onsite water supply system, DOH regulations and/or permits must be reviewed.

This jurisdiction could be particularly pertinent to coastal properties, as it is not uncommon for many coastal properties, particularly those in rural or remote locations, to be serviced by wells. Both the potential pollution of these wells (including from tidal water influences) and increasingly the sufficiency of the capacity of these wells are important considerations for many coastal properties. This is discussed in chapter 4, addressing due diligence in the acquisition of coastal properties.

The DOH's website, with its current regulations, may be found at www.health.state.ri.us/.

The Narragansett Bay Commission

The Narragansett Bay Commission (NBC), formerly known as the Narragansett Bay Water Quality District Commission, is also sometimes overlooked as an environmental regulator, but it is both an important and powerful one. The NBC owns and operates the sewer system treatment facilities at Fields Point in Providence and Bucklin Point in East Providence. Its system services Providence, Johnston, Pawtucket, Central Falls, Cumberland, Lincoln, the northern part of East Providence, and small segments of Cranston and Smithfield.

As such, it issues permits for connection into the sewer system, and it regulates discharges into the sewer system. Its regulatory activity includes enforcement actions and potentially substantial fines for discharges to the system in violation of a facility's permit, or in violation of applicable NBC regulations.

Under its pretreatment program, it requires pretreatment of certain harmful contaminants by businesses. Industries monitored include chemical manufacturers, electroplaters, metal finishers, machine shops, laboratories, laundromats, restaurants, and hospitals.

The NBC also has an impact on development, particularly in areas served by combined sewer overflows, or CSOs (areas where, when during periods of high rain activity, one line may carry overflows of storm water and sewage). CSOs are being phased out, and the NBC will prevent new connections into the CSOs, requiring instead that new lines are run. This understandably increases the cost of development in these areas.

Given the areas that it serves, the impact of the Narragansett Bay Commission on coastal properties is limited, although it cannot be discounted if you are purchasing coastal properties within its jurisdiction, such as Providence.

The NBC's website, which also contains its current regulations, may be found at www.narrabay.com.

Rhode Island Historic Preservation and Heritage Commission

The Rhode Island Historic Preservation and Heritage Commission is another agency often overlooked as a regulator of property, but its impact on properties can be significant. The Commission has statewide jurisdiction, with a mission to protect and preserve historic buildings and structures, historic districts, and archeological sites. Its jurisdiction can be particularly important when new development of coastal properties is at issue, in the event that the property implicates an archeological site or a historic district, or involves a historical structure. For example, development could be precluded on the site, or alteration of a historical structure could be prevented. In chapter 4, dealing with due diligence in acquiring property, I discuss in detail a coastal residential development project that was stopped midstream by the discovery of a Native American archeology site in the midst of the project. The Historic Preservation and Heritage Commission urged that the CRMC permit to construct be revoked, the developer did not prevail in court, and literally millions of dollars are at issue.

The Commission's website can be found at www.preservation.ri.gov.

Rhode Island Coastal Resources Management Council

The program it administers, the Rhode Island Coastal Resources Management Program, has a regulatory enabling act, RI Gen. Laws 46–23–1 *et seq.*, but is primarily reflected in detailed and frequently amended regulations known as the Red Book. The Rhode Island Coastal Resources Management Council (CRMC) is the primary regulator of Rhode Island's coastline and tidal waters. It administers and enforces a very complex and detailed Coastal Resources Management Program that governs virtually every activity at the shoreline, from repair of a dock to an addition to a waterfront single family house to the construction of a marina or a development project on the coast. As I discuss in chapter 4, its jurisdiction is sometimes deceptively wider than may reasonably be anticipated.

The Red Book may be found on the CRMC's website at www.crmc.ri.gov/.

The Coastal Resources Management Council has a professional staff of engineers, biologists, environmental scientists, and marine resource specialists overseen by an executive director and assisted by legal counsel.

The decision-making body of the council is a sixteen-member board appointed by the governor for three-year terms. Members, who serve part time, are citizens who have varying degrees of coastal zone management expertise. While some have environmental or regulatory expertise, such as the director of the Department of Environmental Management or its designee, who serves *ex officio*, others may be private citizens or state or local government representatives.

The Council was created by statute, RI Gen. Laws § 46–23–1 *et seq.*, and its statutory mission is "to preserve, protect, develop, and, where possible, restore the coastal resources of the state for this and succeeding generations through comprehensive and coordinated long range planning and management designed to produce the maximum benefit for society for these coastal resources" (RI Gen. Laws § 46–23–1 [a] [2]). Its statutory authority includes broad powers for planning as well as for enforcement of violations of CRMC policies and procedures. The CRMC has primary jurisdiction over coastal waters and land areas within two hundred feet of the inland edge of a coastal feature, although, as I discuss in chapter 4 and chapter 6, this jurisdiction is often broader depending on the areas and matters at issue. As is also noted there, the CRMC may exercise jurisdiction over wetlands traditionally exercised by the DEM when those wetlands are proximate to the coast.

CRMC permission is required for a broad range of activities within its jurisdiction ranging from new construction to installation of a dock to an addition to a house to the construction of a marina to the alteration of wetlands in the vicinity of the coast. Indeed, as I discuss in chapter 4, CRMC's consent is required for so many activities that property owners are often surprised that regulatory consent may even be necessary. For example, consent may be required to trim trees or cut vegetation, which is not something property owners usually think requires governmental consent when it occurs on their own property. The important thing to understand at this juncture is that if you are within CRMC's jurisdiction, you ignore their rules and regulations (which are extensive) at your peril, including when conducting due diligence for the acquisition of coastal property.

Before leaving this discussion of state regulatory authorities that can impact Rhode Island coastal properties, I want to also provide a listing of relevant Rhode Island land use and environmental statutes that can impact Rhode Island real estate transactions including, obviously, coastal properties. For your convenience, these are included in Table 2A.

Federal Regulators

While there are numerous federal statutes and regulations with jurisdictional authority over environmental and land use regulatory matters that can directly impact Rhode Island coastal properties, I will focus on only two federal regulators, the Environmental Protection Agency (EPA) and the US Army Corps of Engineers, or the Corps. These are the two federal regulator agencies that are primarily encountered in Rhode Island in reference to coastal properties. However, for your reference I have also set forth in Table 2B a listing of federal environmental statutes that may impact Rhode Island real estate transactions involving coastal properties.

Environmental Protection Agency

Region 1 of the federal Environmental Protection Agency administers and enforces numerous federal environmental statutes and regulations in Rhode Island and the other New England states, including the federal Superfund statute. However, in Rhode Island many of the same environmental programs covered under these basic federal programs and statutes have also effectively been delegated to the state, pursuant to which the state promulgates state statutes and regulations that the EPA reviews and accepts if they at least meet the requirements of the federal programs. The net result is that the requirements of the federal statutes and regulations are met by the state statutes and regulations enforced by state authorities.

Nevertheless, the EPA retains the jurisdiction to enforce federal environmental statutes and regulations in Rhode Island, and they will act, including if the state is not taking enforcement action in a particular case that the EPA believes should be pursued.

The EPA and the state enter into Performance Partnership Agreements establishing mutual work plans under goals pertaining to Air, Water,

Communities and Ecosystems, Compliance Assistance and Enforcement, and Open and Effective Government. The most recent partnership agreement is available through a link on EPA's Region 1 website.

This website, which contains substantial useful information, may be found at www.epa.gov/NE/.

United States Army Corps of Engineers

The US Army Corps of Engineers has jurisdiction, and permitting authority, over activities that affect "waters of the United States." This jurisdiction arises under two statutes, Section 404 of the Clean Water Act (33 US. Code 1344), and Section 10 of the Rivers and Harbors Act of 1899 (33 US. Code 403). Section 10 of the Rivers and Harbors Act and Section 404 of the Clean Water Act encompass all navigable waters of the United States, and Section 404 also includes waters, including wetlands, with a sufficient nexus to interstate commerce. This could include isolated wetlands, intermittent streams, and other waters not part of a tributary system to interstate or navigable waters.

With regard to waters under Section 404, in tidal waters the jurisdictional limit of the Corps is the high tide line, for nontidal waters it is the ordinary high-water mark, and for wetlands it is the border of the wetland.

Under Section 10, navigable waters extend to the mean high-water line and include navigable coastal and inland waters, oceans, rivers, lakes, and streams. In Rhode Island, the Corps considers all tidal water and their tributaries to the head of the tide to be navigable waters.

The Army Corps has issued Rhode Island a general permit for certain activities in jurisdictional waters so long as they have only a minimum impact on the marine ecosystem. If the impacted area is less than five thousand square feet, the work may be done without reporting to the Army Corps, provided applicable state permits are obtained. If the impacted area is greater than five thousand square feet but not exceeding one acre, the work will still fall under the general permit, but requires reporting to, and a signoff from, the Army Corps.

There has been considerable controversy over the years as to exactly what constitutes "waters of the United States" and considerable litigation, including at least two US Supreme Court decisions where the Court found the regulatory agencies had exceeded their jurisdiction. In one, the Army Corps relied on the "Migratory Bird Rule" to assert that if a migratory bird might land in an isolated water body, it was waters of the United States. This was derisively referred to by many property rights advocates as the "Glancing Goose Rule," as a goose that may find an isolated mud hole filled with storm water enticing was establishing national regulatory jurisdiction. The Supreme Court found that the "Migratory Bird Rule" went too far (*Solid Waste Agency of Northern Cook County v. United States Army Corps of Engineers*, 531 US 159 [2001]). In another case, the Corps was prevented from regulating "isolated" wetlands (*Rapanos v. United States*, 547 US 715 [2006]).

The controversy continues as the Army Corps and the EPA are now seeking to rewrite the definition of "waters of the United States." They are meeting with opposition that claims they are inappropriately trying to extend their statutory jurisdiction by rule-making.

The important lesson for those purchasing coastal properties or seeking to alter coastal properties is one of caution. You should seek professional wetlands guidance in the event the property at issue is coastal and may be impacted by wetlands.

The website for the Army Corps of Engineers for the New England District may be accessed at www.nae.usace.army.mil/.

Table 2A
Rhode Island Land Use and Environmental Statutes Impacting Real Estate

Administrative Penalties for Environmental Violations, R. I. Gen. Laws § 42–17.6–1 *et seq.*

Air Pollution Episode Control Act. RI Gen. Laws § 23–23.1-1 *et seq.*

Air Pollution, R. I. Gen. Laws § 23–23–1 *et seq.*

Antiquities Act of Rhode Island, R. I. Gen. Laws § 42–45.1–1 *et seq.*

Asbestos Abatement Act, RI Gen. Laws § 23–24.5–1 *et seq.*

Coastal Resources Management Council Enabling Statute, RI Gen. Laws § 46–23–1 *et seq.*

Commercial Leasing and Other Estates, RI Gen. Laws § 34–18.1–1, *et seq.*

Contamination of Drinking Water, RI Gen. Laws § 46–14–1 *et seq.*

Department of Environmental Management Enabling Statute, RI Gen. Laws § 42–17.1–1 *et seq.*

Energy Facility Siting Act, RI Gen. Laws § 42–98–1 *et seq.*

Enforcement of Certain Natural Resource Violations, RI Gen. Laws § 42–17.10–1 *et seq.*

Expedited Permit Process, RI Gen Laws § 42–117–1 *et seq.*

Generation, Transportation, Storage, Treatment, Management and Disposal of Medical Waste, RI Gen. Laws § 23–19.12–1 *et seq.*

Hazardous Substances Act, RI Gen. Laws § 23–24–1 *et seq.*

Hazardous Substances Community Right to Know Act, RI Gen. Laws § 23–24.4–1 *et seq.*

Hazardous Waste Management Act, RI Gen. Laws § 23–19.1–1 *et seq.*

Historic Area Zoning, RI Gen. Laws § 45–24.1–1 *et seq.*

Industrial Property Remediation and Reuse Act, RI Gen. Laws § 23–19.12–1 *et seq.*

Lead Hazard Mitigation, RI Gen. Laws § 42–128.1–1 *et seq.*

Lead Poisoning Prevention Act, RI Gen. Laws § 23–24.6–1 *et seq.*

Leased Land Dwellings, RI Gen. Laws § 34–18.2–1 *et seq.*

Local Health Regulation, RI Gen. Laws § 23–19.2–1 *et seq.*

Mobile and Manufactured Homes, RI Gen. Laws § 31–44–1 *et seq.*

Narragansett Bay Commission Enabling Statute, RI Gen. Laws § 46–25–1 *et seq.*

Oil Pollution Control Act, RI Gen. Laws § 46–5.5.–1 *et seq.*

Refuse Disposal Act, RI Gen. Laws § 23–18.9–1 *et seq.*

Regulation of Out of State Real Estate Sales and Dispositions, RI Gen. Laws § 34–38–1 *et seq.*

Residential Landlord and Tenant Act, RI Gen. Laws § 34–18–1 *et seq.*

Rhode Island Cesspool Act of 2007, RI Gen. Laws § 23–19.15–1 *et seq.*

Rhode Island Comprehensive Planning and Land Use Regulation Act, RI Gen. Laws § 45–22.2–1 *et seq.*

Rhode Island Condominium Act, RI Gen. Laws § 34–36.1–1.01 *et seq.*

Rhode Island Development Impact Fee Act, RI Gen. Laws § 45–22.4–1 *et seq.*

Rhode Island Environmental Compliance Act, RI Gen. Laws § 42–17.8–1 *et seq.*

Rhode Island Groundwater Protection Act, R. I. Gen. Laws § 46–13.1–1 *et seq.*

Rhode Island Historic Preservation and Heritage Commission Enabling Statute, RI Gen. Laws § 42–45–1 *et seq.*

Rhode Island Housing, Maintenance and Occupancy Code, RI Gen. Laws § 45–24.3–1 *et seq.*

Rhode Island Land Development and Subdivision Review Enabling Act of 1992, RI Gen. Laws § 45–23–25 through 45–23–74

Rhode Island Real Estate Time-Share Act, RI Gen. Laws § 34–41–1.01 *et seq.*

Rhode Island Zoning Enabling Act of 1991, RI Gen. Laws § 45–24–27 through 45–24–72

Underground Storage Tanks, RI Gen. Laws § 46–12.1–1 *et seq.*

Table 2B

Federal Environmental Statutes Impacting Real Estate

Antiquities Act, 16 USC §§ 431–433m

Clean Air Act, 42 USC § 7401 *et seq.*

Clean Water Act, 33 USC § 1251 *et seq.*

Coastal Zone Management Act, 16 USC § 1451 *et seq.*

Comprehensive Environmental Response, Compensation and Liability Act, 42 USC § 9601 *et seq.*

Emergency Planning and Community Right-to-Know Act, 42 USC § 11001 *et seq.*

Endangered Species Act, 16 USC § 1531 *et seq.*

Federal Power Act, 16 USC § 791 *et seq.*

Federal Water Pollution Control Amendments (see Clean Water Act)

National Environmental Policy Act, 42 USC § 4321 *et seq.*

National Historic Preservation Act, 16 USC § 470 *et seq.*

Occupational Safety and Health (OSHA), 29 USC § 651 *et seq.*

Oil Pollution Act, 33 USC § 2701 *et seq.*

Pollution Prevention Act, 42 USC § 13101 *et seq.*

Resource Conservation and Recovery Act, 42 USC § 6901 *et seq.*

Rivers and Harbors Act, 33 USC §§ 401–467

Superfund Amendments and Reauthorization Act (see Comprehensive Environmental Response, Compensation and Liability Act)

Toxic Substances Control Act, 15 USC § 2601 *et seq.*

Wild and Scenic Rivers Act, 16 USC §§ 1271–1287

_____

Environmental laws pertaining to public lands and mining have not been included.

CHAPTER 3

Negotiations, Offers, and the Purchase and Sale Agreement

Overview of the Purchase and Sale Process

While most purchasers of coastal property I encounter are experienced in real estate transactions, because some may be first-time buyers and more may be unfamiliar with the customs of real estate sales in Rhode Island, an overview of the process, albeit brief, is appropriate.

In Rhode Island, most residential transactions involve realtors, state licensed real estate brokers, or salespersons (hereinafter sometimes referred to as "realtors") who have access to the statewide multiple listing service where most residential real estate is listed for sale. Realtors are also often involved in commercial transactions, although it is not unusual in commercial transactions to see experienced business people buying and selling commercial properties without listing with or using the services of a realtor.

A transaction, particularly a residential transaction, often begins with an offer, which if accepted results in the preparation of a purchase and sale agreement. For residential transactions, these are generally done by the completion of form documents.

Realtors often use forms adopted and approved by the Rhode Island Board of Realtors. These preprinted forms are particularly ubiquitous in residential real estate transactions. It is also common in residential real estate transactions for the forms to be filled in by the realtors themselves and for the transaction to be negotiated by the realtors on each side of the transaction. In commercial transactions, particularly of any significant size, scope, or complexity, attorneys are often involved in negotiating and drafting offers and purchase and sale agreements.

The Rhode Island Board of Realtor forms are actually good documents, although they must be carefully tailored to the particular transaction, and as discussed below, I generally recommend changes to those documents under a variety of circumstances. Also, when a residential transaction is substantial, with significant complexity, lawyers will often get involved and either negotiate a substantial addendum to the form agreement or create their own purchase and sale agreements.

Once a purchase and sale agreement has been signed, the purchaser will conduct whatever inspections or due diligence the agreement calls for, including without limitation, inspections of the structure for termites or other invasive insects or for structural deficiencies, electrical, plumbing, and/or mechanical deficiencies, the presence of lead, the functionality of the individual sewage disposal system, water wells, etc., to the extent applicable. Some or all of these inspections can be waived by the purchaser. The purchaser will also arrange with a title company for an examination of legal title to the property to ensure it is marketable and free of encumbrances, restrictions, etc. that may impact the use or enjoyment of the property, its ability to be financed, etc. The purchaser will also apply for financing for the acquisition if that is a consideration, which may be subject to a mortgage contingency allowing termination of the transaction if the specified financing is not obtained in the specified time. Upon the appointed time, if all the contingencies have been met, the closing occurs—usually at the offices of a title company or attorney for the buyer, who may also be the title attorney in residential transactions.

While the process appears straightforward, things can, and sometimes do, go wrong. The good news is that most transactions close, and most parties walk away happy. The bad news is that some transactions close, and one or both of the parties walk away unhappy because of something that was not anticipated; other transaction don't close, and some transactions lead to litigation. Much of what follows is intended to foster a happy rather than an unhappy transaction experience.

The discussion that follows assumes that the transaction at issue is a significant financial transaction, in excess of $500,000 in purchase price, and often well in excess of that, and that the transaction has some complexity to it, as many waterfront and water view transactions do.

The Negotiation Process

The most important decision any purchaser must make about the negotiation process is not how much money to initially offer, not how to handle counteroffers, not what maximum purchase price to pay, or not what terms to demand. Rather, the most important decision about the negotiation process is who shall do the negotiating, and it is a question to which too many purchasers give too little thought, or no thought at all.

As indicated, in a typical residential real estate transaction, the realtors often are the negotiators. Some realtors may be excellent negotiators, and some may be terrible negotiators. And you may not know what category your realtor falls into until it is too late.

Another dynamic of the transaction, in my experience, is that realtors often want all communications to go through them. I have in fact seen this very frequently. This often makes sense in the garden-variety house real estate transaction, where buyers and sellers may be first-time buyers or generally inexperienced in real estate matters. In such cases, the role assumed by realtors can be helpful to the transaction. However, in significant coastal property transactions, the purchasers and sellers are often very experienced in real estate and/or business and financial matters and more than capable of dealing directly with one another if they so choose—and many do. I have represented purchasers in waterfront property transactions who were venture capitalists, investment bankers, and CEOs, and I can tell you that they were highly skilled negotiators who needed absolutely no help from brokers in negotiating complex transaction issues.

What works in garden-variety real estate transactions is not the best model for expensive coastal property transactions, whether for residential or commercial uses. For these types of transactions, I recommend purchasers engage an experienced lawyer, and I personally think it is beneficial if the seller also engage a lawyer. Some purchasers may think it would be an advantage to be represented by counsel and for the seller not to be represented by counsel. After years of transaction experience, I disagree.

The simple fact is that often a seller or his or her realtor may object to conditions required by purchaser's counsel because they do not fully understand the conditions or why purchaser is insisting on them, while an experienced seller's counsel may readily agree because he or she would want the same thing if he or she were representing a purchaser and because he or she understands it poses no material detriment to his or her client, and may well recognize that not agreeing would be a deal breaker. That is not to say that some lawyers can't be difficult (I am being charitable here, and note the use of the double negative to pad the blow). However, my experience has led me to always want the smartest lawyer possible on the other side of the transaction. The net result will be an improved transaction.

Accordingly, for any purchaser of a significant coastal property, I recommend the purchaser engage experienced counsel, and I encourage the seller to do the same. And when the purchaser has engaged counsel, it is highly likely that the seller will do so, as the tenor of the transaction will have changed, and a seller who is not a lawyer and not comatose will likely conclude that legal representation is required.

The attorneys will generally conduct all negotiations between themselves, in consultation with their respective clients. That is an effective model with one caveat. Sometimes it makes good sense for purchaser and seller to have face-to-face discussions, particularly if sensitive business or financial issues are involved, and (I emphasize the conjunctive) the parties are sophisticated businesspersons. Some years back I represented a sophisticated investor in buying waterfront property from a property owner who was an experienced real estate lawyer, and between them they came up with a transaction that not only worked, but was extremely complicated. Trying to negotiate that between intermediaries would have been difficult. Discussions between the principals would preferably be with counsel, for the primary purpose of not making agreements that inadvertently implicated some legal issues that the principals did not recognize.

With regard to the negotiation process, it is highly recommended that the purchaser not send written notes, letters, or e-mails to the seller during this process. If the transaction results in a dispute, it may be argued that this has become a part of the terms of the transaction. For example, a purchaser writes to his seller during the negotiation process that he will only agree to give the seller a right to lease a carriage house on the property being purchased after the closing at a specified below market rate if seller reduces the purchase price to two million dollars. Negotiations continue between counsel, and subsequently the transaction closes for a two million dollar purchase price. The seller claims the right to lease the carriage house, and purchaser asserts the price reduction resulted from a concession purchaser made that is not spelled out in the purchase and sale agreement. Litigation ensues. Who wins is an open question, but we know the litigating lawyers didn't lose. It is not uncommon to have disputes after a purchase and sale agreement has been signed and before closing, and sometimes e-mails and other writings can be misinterpreted and fuel the controversy. Please leave the writing to the lawyers.

The Offer

While the Rhode Island Board of Realtors has an offer form, many realtors use their own offer form, which realtors often prepare when a prospective purchaser is interested in submitting an offer to purchase. There is no requirement to submit an offer as opposed to a proposed purchase and sale agreement containing the terms and conditions on which the purchaser wishes to purchase the property. An argument for using the offer form is that it is truncated, quicker to prepare, and if it is unclear whether the terms of purchase will be acceptable, the offer is a quicker and easier way to determine whether there may be a meeting of the minds. It is also sometimes argued that if there is substantial interest in the property, it may be best to get a quick offer in to see if the prospective purchase can tie up the property and freeze out the other buyers.

While those arguments may have validity, the reality is that offers are usually nonbinding, nothing precludes a purchaser from collecting several offers and from using them to negotiate better terms and conditions, and acceptance of an offer does not guarantee a purchase and sale agreement will be executed. Also, because purchase and sale agreements are more detailed, the offer often does not contain all of the material terms and condition of the transaction, only the most obvious ones such as purchase price, time of closing, what personal property or furnishings transfer with the sale, etc.

My personal preference is to ignore the offer and move the transaction forward by submitting a purchase and sale agreement for consideration by the seller with all the proposed terms and conditions of sale. One reason for this position is that the fewer documents between the parties, the better. More documents can lead to more misunderstandings or, in the event of litigation, to the opportunity for one side to characterize a transaction in a way that the parties did not intend.

To those that are so concerned about losing the perfect property by not being the first in the door with an offer, I would suggest that what has been said about perfect investments applies to perfect properties—they are like buses, and there will be another one along in fifteen minutes. In other words, it is usually not a good idea for a purchaser to approach a negotiation from the perspective that the property is absolutely perfect, and the purchaser must have it.

Such a purchaser will likely overpay and ignore red flags during due diligence that could come back to haunt the then-owner.

If an offer is submitted, I strongly suggest a purchaser put a strict limit on the effective date of the offer, and make it clear that no binding legal obligation to purchase the property shall arise absent execution of a purchase and sale agreement. Many forms of offers do indicate that it is "subject to execution of a formal purchase and sale agreement" or similar language. As will be apparent from the discussion below concerning how real estate negotiations can go from bad to worse to litigation, such language may not be enough to avoid characterizing an accepted offer or a term sheet as an enforceable contract. I suggest a purchaser include clear and unequivocal language so even if it ends up in front of the world's worst jury or judge, the purchaser has a fair chance of prevailing. The following language is one suggestion:

"This Offer shall automatically expire by its terms at 6:00 p.m. on [insert specified date], at which time it shall be null and void and of no further effect, whether or not it is "accepted" by the Seller before or after that date. No legally binding obligation to purchase the Property shall arise by virtue of this Offer, regardless of whether it is purportedly accepted, and no legally binding obligation between the parties to purchase the Property shall arise unless and until a mutually agreeable Purchase and

Sale Agreement has been duly authorized, executed and delivered by Buyer and Seller."

The obvious concern is that no contractual purchase obligations arise unless and until both parties have consented to such contractual obligations. This concern is not idle, as the discussion below of negations in a real estate transaction gone terribly wrong will demonstrate.

The Purchase and Sale Agreement

If the suggestions set forth in this chapter have been followed, the purchase and sale agreement will be handled by attorneys representing purchaser and seller. For residential property, the Board of Realtors' standard form purchase and sale agreement may be used, or the attorneys may utilize a more sophisticated document if that is what is appropriate to the transaction. Given that contract provisions should be added or customized as the nature and scope of the transaction requires (which will be fact-specific at it pertains to the property in question and what is intended with regard to the use of the property), I will provide general comments on the form purchase and sale agreement on the assumption that the purchase involves a single-family residence on a coastal property and does not involve a tear-down and rebuilding of the structure or other radical alteration. Such planned activities will require carefully tailored provisions in the purchase and sale agreement. And, consideration here will only be given to issues about which a purchaser should be concerned. Seller issues are addressed in chapter 10.

Parties

While a title search is generally initiated only after a purchase and sale agreement has been signed, it is important that the party signing the agreement as seller is in fact the owner of the property, or else you may not have an enforceable document. For example, the property may be owned by husband and wife, they are estranged, and only the husband signs, saying he is the sole owner. Or the husband and wife sign individually, but the property was put into a trust some years back for estate planning purposes. One of the things the listing agent should confirm is the ownership of the property, but oversights and mistakes do happen. A quick search of the municipality's online real estate tax database or similar records may be helpful initially in confirming you have an agreement signed by the actual owners of the property and all of the owners of the property. But those records could be out of date or otherwise incorrect.

Deposits

The form agreement provides that deposits are held by the listing realtor firm in escrow. When it is a significant transaction, I often provide that the deposits be held by the title insurance company that will be running the title and issuing the title policy for the purchaser, and I often do a formal escrow agreement to be signed by the seller, the purchaser, and the title company as escrow agent to define the terms of the escrow. This can be particularly important in the event of a dispute or litigation.

Mortgage Contingency

The purchaser should pay careful attention to this provision if the transaction is contingent on financing and ensure it specifies what constitutes acceptable financing and that it provides sufficient time to obtain it. Market conditions vary, and some properties are harder to finance than others, so a purchaser should do a little homework before completing this provision.

Disclosures

Receipt of the disclosure documents by the purchaser is acknowledged in the purchase and sale agreement. However, those documents are not deemed a part of the contract for purposes of a suit to enforce the contract, should that become necessary, and a purchaser may therefore want to incorporate them by reference in the agreement, just in case the transaction goes badly. Of course, the seller may resist this for the same reason.

Possession and Condition of the Property

My comments assume this is a purchase transaction that does not involve a tear-down of the structure or a substantial renovation of the structure. In the event of such a proposed transaction, the purchaser may want to consider altering this provision to address a fire or casualty that destroys the structure prior to the closing, providing not for termination, but for seller's obligation to use insurance proceeds to demolish the remainder of the structure and remove the debris from the site. However, in this regard, be careful that you know whether or not applicable regulations would allow rebuilding in the event of a complete destruction of the structure. In such a circumstance, a purchaser may be well-advised to require the seller to procure full replacement cost insurance and debris removal coverage (if either or both are not already in place) and to give the purchaser the option of terminating the transaction or proceeding to closing in the event of the casualty. That way, the purchaser can ensure that under the circumstances, rebuilding will be allowed. The agreement can provide that evidence of the insurance be provided by a current certificate of the insurer. Also, to the extent the purchaser is named as an additional insured, make sure to request a "cross liability" or severability provision, so-called, insuring any claims by one insured against another insured under the policies.

Personal Property and Fixtures

Fixtures usually convey with the real estate, while personal property generally does not unless expressly included in the transaction. Under Rhode Island law, fixtures are defined by statute for commercial property, but not for residential property. Accordingly, case law must be consulted. While the definition of *fixtures* established by the Rhode Island Supreme Court required that to be a fixture, its removal must cause injury to the estate, that view was long ago abandoned by the court. The court explained:

> We are aware that it has been held in some cases that, in order to give chattels the character of fixtures, they must be so affixed to the realty that they cannot be removed without physical injury thereto; but we think the better opinion, as well as the better reason, is the other way, and in favor of regarding everything as a

fixture which has been attached to the realty, with a view to en-hance the value thereof, and for the purpose of being permanent-ly used in connection therewith...We can see no reason whatever why such fixtures are not as much a part of the realty as radiators, water faucets, set tubs, bath tubs, and bowls, portable furnaces connected with hot-air pipes for heating the building, storm doors and storm windows window blinds, whether inside or outside, fire grates, pumps, mantels, and such other things as are annexed to the freehold with a view to the improvement thereof. All of these things, though mere chattels before their annexation to the free-hold, are no longer such after their annexation, any more than the other materials which go to make up the house, but then become part and parcel of the real estate, and the mere fact that they can be removed therefrom without physical injury to the freehold does not change their character as between the vendor and vendee of the realty. (*Canning v. Owen*, 48 A. 1033, 1035–1036, 22 RI 624, 630–31 [RI 1901])

At times there may be disputes as to what constitutes personal property as opposed to a fixture. To the extent the purchaser has expectations as to certain items coming with the property, those items should be clearly specified in the purchase and sale agreement. Controversy can arise over such items as chandeliers, wall sconces, whether electrified or not, cande-labras, decorative mirrors that may be attached or even built into walls, etc. The grander the home, potentially the larger the issue. And as dis-cussed in chapter 9, from a seller's perspective, this should be addressed in the sales listing process.

Inspections

The ten-day period provided in the form purchase and sale agreement may well be inadequate for any property with a significant structure or structures located on it, or for a property with complex site conditions or one requiring extensive site work after the closing. The time frame should accordingly be extended to an appropriate period. These inspections should be tied in with overall due diligence, discussed in detail in chapter

4. To the extent you are doing extensive due diligence, such as records review of CRMC files, municipal zoning and building inspection records, DEM files, etc., a purchaser may well want to have the inspection period for structural, mechanical, plumbing, sewage disposal systems, water wells, etc. be coterminous with the due diligence period. For example, you may discover information during the due diligence period that requires further inspection of the individual sewage disposal system or the water supply wells, etc. As further discussed in chapter 4, to the extent extensive due diligence is contemplated, as, for example, invasive testing of soil or groundwater, the purchase and sale agreement should address this specifically.

Default

The default provisions in the form purchase and sale agreement allow the seller to retain the deposit in the event of the purchaser's breach and to sue the purchaser to require the purchaser to buy the property (what is known as suing for specific performance) or to sue for damages. Given that disputes are not uncommon in real estate transactions, and litigation can be costly and time-consuming, a purchaser may well want to consider limiting the seller's remedy to retention of the deposit in the event of a breach, as well as, perhaps, the purchaser tendering to the seller any inspection reports or studies it may have done with regard to the property. To the extent the work product, which the purchaser is responsible for paying for, addresses issues pertaining to the property in which other buyers may be interested, there is value in getting such reports.

With regard to seller's default, a purchaser may want to consider as a remedy return of its deposit or specific performance—the right to force the seller to sell the property to the purchaser. The purchaser's concern is that he or she does not want the seller to get a better offer after the purchase and sale agreement is signed and breach the agreement to sell to a higher bidder. The right of specific performance could thwart such a seller tactic. Alternatively, instead of specific performance, the purchaser may want to consider a remedy involving return of the deposit and reimbursement for any out-of-pocket expenses incurred in the transaction, particularly if, as a result of the seller's conduct or otherwise, the purchaser has lost interest in the property. Since due diligence costs of a purchaser can involve not only legal fees, but engineering fees, architectural fees, environmental engineering fees, etc., repayment of out-of-pocket costs could be an important remedy, particularly if it can be done without litigation.

Amendment

The form purchase and sale agreement provides that "[t]his Agreement may not be changed, modified, or amended in whole or in part except in writing, signed by all the parties." That is probably sufficient, although a purchaser may wish to add something like the following to ensure there is no misunderstanding:

"Such an amendment shall only be deemed effective if it is denominated 'Amendment to Purchase and Sale Agreement,' and no e-mails, correspondence, or verbal discussions between and/or among the parties and/or their representatives shall constitute such an amendment."

Additionally, after the purchase and sale agreement has been signed, if the parties undertake negotiations for an amendment of the agreement, I recommend similar language be used in letters or e-mails discussing the potential terms of such an amendment. For example, as I write this, I am involved in discussions pertaining to an executed purchase and sale agreement for a multimillion dollar sale of coastal property for commercial uses. I have used language comparable to the following provision in letters and e-mails that discuss whether the transaction may be restructured by amendment to the purchase and sale agreement and the potential terms of such an amendment, in order to avoid any misunderstandings if the transaction later collapses:

As more specifically set forth in prior correspondence on this issue, no changes in the terms and conditions of the Agreement shall be effective unless and until a document expressly denominated as an Amendment to the Agreement is executed and delivered by the parties, and no interim correspondence, such as letters like this or e-mails, shall be deemed, individually or with other correspondence or e-mails, to constitute such an amendment.

You may even consider putting that in boldface in your correspondence.

And if you are wondering why the heightened concern on this issue, consider the following decision from a federal circuit court of appeals, upholding a trial court decision that a one page, nine paragraph, 205 word document labeled "Final Proposal" constituted a legally enforceable contract for a complex multimillion dollar real estate transaction.

How Negotiations Can Go Terribly Wrong

An example of what can go very wrong in real estate negotiations arose in the context of a developer negotiating with the owner of land on which the developer wanted to build a large mixed-use project. The parties negotiated over the course of several years, but could not agree on terms. The developer was primarily interested in buying the land, and the owner wanted to lease the land as it did not want to sell for a number of years.

After extensive negotiations, the parties finally agreed on the outline of a business proposal. When I say outline, I mean just that. They inked a one page, 205 word, nine paragraph document labeled a "Final Proposal." The proposal involved the developer developing a multimillion dollar project under a "ground lease" for initial rental of one hundred thousand dollars per month. The document included language that the developer was to prepare "a legal agreement" for the other side's review "to finalize the agreement." The document further stated that "[t]he above terms are hereby accepted by the parties subject only to approval of the terms and conditions of a formal agreement."

Incredibly, at trial a jury found that this document was a legally enforceable contract, the developer was guilty of anticipatory breach, and the developer owed the property owner more than fifteen million dollars in damages. That decision was upheld by the Ninth Circuit Court of Appeals (see *First National Mortgage Company v. Federal Realty Investment Trust*, 631 F.3d 1058 [9th Cir. 2011]).

Anyone familiar with real estate development knows that ground leases are complex documents that can easily take months to negotiate before signing. When that transaction was finally documented, it likely would have involved a contract of well over a hundred pages, including detailed provisions to make it a financeable deal. Yet, this term sheet was found by a trial court and appellate court to be a legally enforceable contract for the development of a multimillion dollar project on land that the developer did not own.

Moreover, the developer quite properly alleged that one of the essential terms of the transaction was missing, the length of the ground lease, and without an essential term the agreement was not enforceable. The court found that the lease term could be inferred because under the proposal the developer had the right to force a purchase of the property after ten years, so the court concluded that the term of the lease was ten years. (By the way, a ground lease of ten years for a multimillion dollar development project may well not have been a financeable document unless the purchase option was ironclad, it could not be stayed by bankruptcy provisions and in the event the purchase option could not be exercised for whatever reason, the lease would continue for at least a fifty-year term—all highly unlikely under the scenario in the case at issue.)

I find the lower court decision, upheld on appeal, to be simply stunning. The jury clearly could not have understood the sophisticated nature of the proposed transaction. That being said, it is an important lesson to all deal-makers. Be very careful what is put in writing, and be very careful what is signed.

Although the case at issue did not arise in Rhode Island and is not binding case law in Rhode Island, it is nevertheless highly instructive on how real estate purchase and sale transactions, as well as lease transactions, must be carefully handled.

Also, be very careful about what may be communicated verbally. For example, in one case in Rhode Island, a trial court found that a seller who appeared to reach verbal (not written, but verbal) agreement with a purchaser, but who later accepted and signed another offer, was actually bound by his verbal discussion. While that case was subsequently overturned by the Rhode Island Supreme Court, it nevertheless is an indication of how careful you have to be (see *Smith v. Boyd*, 553 A.2d 131 [RI 1989]). Under the statute of frauds applicable in most jurisdictions, contracts for the sale of real estate or for the lease of real estate for longer than one year must be evidenced in writing (RI Gen. Laws Section 9–1–4). The difficulty comes when someone claims that substantive discussions, which are supported to some degree by notes, e-mails, messages, etc., can form a contract.

Moreover, it is quite possible that a court could find that a signed agreement by the parties could be altered by the exchange of e-mails between the parties. It is also possible that a court could find that verbal discussions, evidenced by "some" writing, not a formal contract by any means, but "some" writing, may be found to amend the contract.

And even more caution must be urged, as the contract between two deal-makers, say a buyer and a seller, may be found to have been altered or amended by the agent of one or both of the parties. In Rhode Island, as in many states, the disclosed agent of a principal can bind the principal. Accordingly, the realtor of the seller, as the seller's disclosed agent, could say or do something that could bind the seller. I have actually seen instances where a realtor has written to a buyer and the buyer's agent stating what the seller would do, even indicating the e-mail was from the agent and the seller, all without the seller's prior knowledge or consent.

Instructive is a Rhode Island Supreme Court decision decided in 1962, *Cuddigan v. List*, 177 A. 2d 195 (RI 1962). In this case, a realtor's signature on a deposit receipt and his tendering of keys to a purchaser was found to be a contract binding the owner, who later tried to accept another offer.

The listing realtor called the owner to see if he would accept a sale price below listing price, the owner agreed, the buyer tendered a deposit and was given a receipt by the realtor detailing the transaction and also providing as follows: "Important: This deposit accepted subject to the approval of seller—and buyer—to conditions contained in an agreement of sale to be submitted by _____" (The party to prepare the sales agreement was not identified and left blank). The sales agent also handed the keys to the buyer and said the property was his. The court found the deposit receipt met the requirements of the statute of frauds and that the trial justice was justified in finding that a binding agreement arose when the sales agent gave the buyer the signed receipt, accepted the deposit, tendered the keys, and said the property was his.

Well, so much for that important provision that the transaction was subject to a satisfactory purchase and sale agreement.

This decision was relied upon by the First Circuit Court of Appeals in a similar case, where a seller told his broker that he accepted a buyer's offer, the broker prepared and sent the sales agreement to the buyer (who returned it signed with a deposit check), and then later sued the seller when the seller purported to accept a higher offer. The court found that the broker did not need a written authorization from the owner to bind the owner to a purchase transaction, and a verbal acceptance by telephone conveyed to the broker was sufficient to enable the broker to bind the owner in the purchase transaction (see *Leach v. Crucible Center Company*, 388 F.2d 176 [1st Cir. 1968]).

In another Rhode Island trial court decision, the court found that a real estate agent who was given a signed listing agreement from a property owner with an exclusive right to sell the property (meaning that the agent would receive a commission no matter who procured the buyer) could bind the seller to a contract (*MacKnight v. Pansey*, 412 A. 2d 236 [RI 1980]). That decision was overturned by the Rhode Island Supreme Court, holding that a listing agreement did not give the agent the authority to bind the seller to a contract. Nevertheless, in reaching its decision, the supreme court reviewed the *Cuddigan* decision, agreeing that an agent could bind the seller when the seller had been advised by the agent of the offer by telephone, the seller had accepted the offer, and the acceptance was conveyed to the buyer, who signed the agreement and tendered a deposit that was accepted and for which a receipt was issued. (In *MacKnight v. Pansey*, the court found that a purchase and sale agreement signed by the seller's agent was not sufficient to bind the seller, despite the fact that verbal exchanges may have made the buyers feel as though they had a binding deal, because the realtor was not given the seller's authority to bind the seller.)

By statute, Rhode Island has addressed the agency issues arising under realtor relationships with clients (see RI Gen. Laws 5–20.6–1 *et seq.*).

So these cases are very fact specific, and it is necessary to exercise caution regarding potential contract formation when significant property transactions are at issue. For these reasons, it is important that if the lawyer has the opportunity to be involved in the transaction before the purchase and sale agreement is signed, the attorney should be careful to take control of the drafting of the purchase and sale agreement whenever possible and keep the written communications between lawyers. Also, by maintaining all client discussions and communications between only the client and his or her lawyer, there is no question as to the preservation of lawyer-client privilege, which could be particularly important if the transaction results in a lawsuit.

CHAPTER 4

Due Diligence

There is perhaps no more important part of the property acquisition process for a purchaser than the due diligence inquiry. While the process can be relatively straightforward for the normal residential purchase transaction, often involving only a housing inspection report, it can be far more complicated for the acquisition of a significant coastal property, particularly if the purchaser intends new construction, a substantial rehabilitation, or in-water or waterfront construction or improvements.

The purpose of due diligence is for the purchaser to determine the condition of the property being acquired, its permitted uses, whether the property complies with applicable zoning, land use, and other legal requirements, and whether the purchaser can do with the property what he intends. A successful due diligence inquiry can save a purchaser costly surprises as well as disasters that literally deprive the purchaser of the benefit of its bargain.

Consider a situation mentioned in the introduction. An intelligent, cautious couple sought to purchase a lovely coastal lot near the water. They made it a condition of their purchase and sale agreement that the lot be buildable and, as evidence of that, they provided in the contract that they must be issued a permit from the Rhode Island Department of Environmental Management (DEM) for an individual sewage disposal system (ISDS) before they would be required to purchase the lot. When the permit was issued by the DEM, they purchased the property and began constructing their house, installing a foundation and undertaking construction of their ISDS. Someone then complained to the DEM that the property was largely wetlands. That of course could not be, since the DEM could not issue a permit for construction of an ISDS in wetlands, right? Well, in this case, wrong. The same environmental agency that issued them the permit for their ISDS next issued them a cease and desist order because their foundation and ISDS were located in wetlands. The permit for the ISDS was improvidently granted. The couple was ordered to remove the foundation and ISDS. Litigation ensues, the order is upheld, and the foundation and partially constructed ISDS were removed.

Fast forward approximately twenty years, during which there was even more litigation, and my former firm was subsequently asked to represent the couple in seeking issuance of permits from the then-regulator, the Coastal Resources Management Council. We were denied a permit for construction of the house. After extensive negotiations with the CRMC staff, after agreeing to put most of the property under a preservation easement, allowing room to build only a small residential dwelling and driveway on the property, and after getting a positive CRMC staff recommendation, the couple was nevertheless denied a permit by the full council after hearing. That denial was appealed to the superior court, arguing that there was no properly admissible evidence in the record to support the decision, and the court reversed the CRMC. This was, of course, a victory for the property owners, but at what cost?

Consider a more recent and even more dramatic example of what can go wrong with regard to the acquisition and development of coastal properties:

An experienced developer owned two waterfront lots on Ocean Road in Narragansett, Rhode Island. He decided to build a luxury waterfront home on one of the lots. The developer constructed a three-story home that included a rooftop cabana with a spa tub and wet bar, marketed the house, and entered into a contract to sell it for $1,800,000. Unfortunately for the developer, the house was constructed on neighboring property, not on the developer's land. The neighboring property was held in trust to be used as a public park and open space, and to the extent any improvements were constructed on it, the trust required that the then-trustees must pay $1,500,000 million to a hospital. Understandably, the trust ordered the structure removed. Litigation ensured, and the Rhode Island Supreme Court upheld the trial court's decision that the house must be moved to the developer's neighboring lot, at a cost of between $300,000 to $400,000, since the house encroached on 13,000 square feet, or approximately 6 percent of the trust's 4.5 acres (*Rose Nulman Park Foundation v. Four Twenty Corp.*, No. 2013–68–Appeal [Rhode Island June 13, 2014]).

It appears the error arose from a survey plan that was prepared for the developer, incorrectly showing that the house was located on the developer's property. The problem was that the survey plan was prepared to a Class III standard. According to the Rhode Island Supreme Court decision, "[T]o the extent that property lines are reflected on such plans [i.e. Class III], they are to be regarded as pictorial only, unless such boundaries are also certified to a Class I, Class II, or Class V standard" (*Id.* at n.4).

Interestingly, the trial court found the developer was justified in relying on the Class III site plan, and while the court did not disagree with that finding, it observed in a footnote that it was curious that an experienced developer was not aware of the infirmities of a Class III survey.

The lesson here is clear. Not only is it prudent for a purchaser to get a Class I survey when acquiring a property, certainly when new construction is planned, it is also important to understand exactly what the due diligence material you pay for actually says and doesn't say.

Organization of Due Diligence Activities

The first questions one confronts in undertaking due diligence activities are who should be overseeing the activities and what activities should be conducted. Addressing the second question first may actually provide guidance for determining who should be overseeing the activities.

What should be done for a reasonable due diligence inquiry will very much depend on what type of property is being acquired, in what location, and for what purposes. Is it an existing structure that will be used "as is," without expansion, construction of new structures, etc.? Is it vacant land that will undergo new construction? Is it an existing structure that must be substantially rehabilitated or perhaps expanded? Is it being acquired for residential purposes, commercial purposes, or industrial uses? Is it located on or adjacent to a water body? Is it in a sensitive environmental area?

The more intensive the proposed use of the site, the more due diligence will be required, and the more extensive the assistance that will be required to conduct the due diligence. If the property is an existing single-family residence that will not be expanded or extensively renovated, due diligence may be relatively limited and capable of being conducted in a short time frame under the supervision of the owner or his counsel. Little more may be implicated than a detailed inspection of the structure and records review. If new construction is envisioned, and the property is in a sensitive, highly regulated area, such as the oceanfront, or on a tidal pond or salt marsh, then due diligence could take months. In this case, the due diligence may be supervised by an experienced contractor, developer, or architect with the assistance of lawyers, wetlands biologists, and engineers. Such activities could include detailed zoning, subdivision, and land use analysis, wetlands mapping, environmental site assessment, subsurface conditions analysis, etc.

Accordingly, at the outset the prospective purchaser should know what is intended with regard to the property. Buying an existing structure with the idea that you may build something different in the future argues strongly for full due diligence activities now to ensure you can do what you intend in the future. If you simply do not know, but want to acquire the property, that is fine, but understand you are running the risk that you may later decide to do something that you subsequently learn is prohibited.

Coastal Threats

I would also suggest that any due diligence inquiry address the threshold question as to whether or not the purchaser in fact wants to own and inhabit a coastal property. Living on the coast is not without its own perils, including the impacts of hurricanes, flooding, and erosion. In this regard, I would recommend the potential purchaser review a guide published by the Rhode Island Coastal Resources Management Council that effectively addresses the hazards that may impact coastal properties. Known as the Rhode Island Coastal Property Guide, it is available on the CRMC website and will be referred to in this book as the CRMC Coastal Guide. It provides a good, if sobering, presentation detailing the potential threats to coastal properties.

For example, a purchaser may want to review the CRMC's Shoreline Change Maps to determine if the property under consideration is in an area that is subject to significant erosion. By showing historic erosion, the maps suggest the course of future erosion, which may or may not materially impact a property. That may be an important data point for the property at issue.

Simple due diligence activities can be overseen by the purchaser or his lawyer, or perhaps the contractor or architect. More complex due diligence analysis may be supervised by an experienced developer or contractor and/or an architectural and engineering firm. The important point is to have someone designated for oversight and supervision, as often the time to conduct such activities is limited, and unsupervised projects can be both inefficient and ineffective.

In order to provide the most benefit to readers with varying purposes in acquiring coastal properties, I will list various types of real estate and environmental due diligence inquiries and provide brief discussion as to important considerations for each of these categories. Prospective purchasers, or their advisors, will necessarily have to pick and choose what is significant or insignificant for the respective property under inquiry.

Real Estate Due Diligence Inquiries

The Real Estate Disclosure Form
One of the first stops for a purchaser on the path of due diligence is a careful examination of the seller's disclosure form, required to be submitted not later than at the time of the signing of the purchase and sale agreement for transactions involving vacant land or residential property of

one to four units. The disclosure obligation is mandated by the Real Estate Sales Disclosures Act, RI Gen. Laws 5–20.8–1 *et seq.*

The Disclosure Act mandates not less than thirty-five required disclosures, all of which are to be to the seller's best knowledge. These disclosures range from the age of the home and the roof, whether or not there exists a working chimney, fireplaces, or wood burning stove, the types of heating and/or air conditioning systems, the company who conducted any termite, pest, or radon testing and the results of such testing, and the condition of the structure itself and its plumbing. Other required disclosures include the property's zoning, flood plain level, the existence of lead paint or hazardous materials such as asbestos, the type of deed to be conveyed, fire damage, as well as any other miscellaneous disclosure the seller may find appropriate. Typically, psychological defects, such as deaths in the home or sightings of apparitions, must be specifically requested by a purchaser.

Disclosure obligations are discussed more extensively in chapter 9, dealing with a property owner's preparation to sell a coastal property. However, from a purchaser's perspective, several essential points should be made here about remedies for a seller's failure to disclose and about the extent of a purchaser's due diligence obligations versus the extent of a seller's disclosure obligations as well as a broker's disclosure obligations.

The Disclosure Act provides a one hundred dollar civil fine as a penalty for each instance of a seller's failure to disclose a matter required to be disclosed under the Act, and the Rhode Island Supreme Court has held that the Disclosure Act does not confer on a purchaser a private cause of action to sue a seller for damages for such a failure to disclose (*Stebbins v. Wells*, 818 A. 2d 711 ([RI 2003]). In that case, which is an important coastal property case, the issue was whether the seller, the seller's real estate agent, and the buyer's real estate agent had a duty to disclose the impact of coastal erosion of the property, which the buyer alleged was significantly more severe than normal erosion. As I discuss in more detail in chapter 9, the failure of a seller to disclose a severe deficient condition may constitute a basis for a lawsuit against the seller for negligent omission or negligence. This could also result in a potential suit against real estate agents for negligent omission, negligence, or breach of fiduciary duty for failure to disclose known information about a severe deficient condition.

In *Stebbins v. Wells*, 766 A. 2d 369 (RI 2001), the court was confronted with a lawsuit by a purchaser of coastal property who contended that the seller, her broker, and the buyer's broker failed to disclose that the property was severely impacted by erosion. The purchaser alleged that he was looking for coastal property in Little Compton, and his broker showed them oceanfront property. He told his broker he would not consider it because ocean erosion would adversely impact his investment. His broker then showed him a riverfront property on brackish water near where the river met the ocean. The purchaser acquired the property and not long after found it was subject to severe erosion—ten feet in the last ten years—after the seller had cut down vegetation. The purchaser also learned that the seller was aware of the problem, and that the purchaser's broker was aware of the problem because the purchaser's broker had previously owned the property for ten years, and she knew that the fact of severe erosion would materially impact the decision to purchase the property (in Rhode Island, six degrees of separation may be quite an overstatement!).

The court found that there was no evidence of misrepresentation by any of the defendants, and that Rhode Island largely followed the rule of *caveat emptor* (let the buyer beware). The court also noted that the buyer had a duty to inspect and inquire about the extent of erosion, given he was buying waterfront property, and that erosion is a natural condition, and its "mere existence cannot be considered a defect for purposes of the disclosure statute" (*Id* at 373). That being said, the court also said that one of the exceptions to the rule of *caveat emptor* in Rhode Island is "passive concealment by the seller of defective realty" (*Id.*). This exception requires a seller or agent "to disclose in situations where he or she has special knowledge not apparent to the buyer and is aware that the buyer is acting under a misapprehension as to facts which would be important to the buyer and would probably affect its decision" (*Id. Wiederholdv. Smith*, 203 Ga. App. 877, 418 S.E. 2d 141, 143 [Ga. Ct. App. 1992]).

The court then remanded the case to the trial court to determine at trial whether the erosion was so severe that it required the seller and agents to disclose this information to the purchaser. The court's subsequent holding in that second case is discussed in detail in chapter 10 as it has material bearing on a seller's disclosure obligations, as well as on the disclosure obligations of real estate brokers. A review of that discussion may also be helpful to a purchaser who questions whether appropriate disclosure was provided with regard to his purchase and what remedies may be available for nondisclosure.

Inspections Set Forth in Standard Form Purchase Agreement

The Rhode Island Association of Realtors standard form purchase agreements set forth many of the standard inspections that a purchaser would be prudent to conduct, including lead inspection, private water well inspection, on-site sewage system inspection, wetlands and flood plains, termites and pests, physical and mechanical, and hazardous substances. While there are opportunities to waive such inspections, this should not be lightly done, and in any event certain testing, such as private potable well water supply, is required by state law as set forth below under environmental due diligence. As also discussed below, to the extent the property is served by a cesspool, it is subject to phase out. In addition to these, a typical home inspection may well encompass such matters as mold, water infiltration, and asbestos, and the physical condition of the structure, as also discussed below.

Physical Property

This inquiry essentially focuses on the parcel or real estate itself. It includes a confirmation of ownership—remember, if you are not dealing with the record owner of the property, you may well not have an enforceable contract. This inquiry also involves the location of the property, legal description, and area and configuration (some properties may be located in different municipalities, which adds complexity to the analysis). What improvements are on the property? Are there offsite improvements that serve the property, such as a communal sewage disposal system? Is there frontage on a public road and legal access, and are these features in conformance with zoning and subdivision regulations?

Is the property a separate tax lot or lots of record? Is there parking as required by municipal regulations? If parking is legally adequate, is it functionally adequate for the parcel? Were the structures built before 1974? If so, asbestos may be an issue. Is the property located in a flood zone? This last question is extremely significant, given the revisions to the flood zone maps and changes in flood insurance, which have significantly increased the costs of certain waterfront properties. This is discussed in detail in chapter 5.

Zoning, Subdivision, and Land Use

A zoning analysis is important for existing properties, and it is critical for properties that are intended for new construction or substantial rehabilitation or expansion. First, you will want to know if your property is a valid and conforming use under the current zoning ordinances. If it is not, it may be an illegal use, or it may be a valid and subsisting nonconforming use, which although not in conformance with the current zoning ordinances, may nevertheless continue to be used for its purposes, and is "grandfathered" under the zoning ordinance. This happens, for example, when a use predated the zoning ordinance and is noncompliant with the subsequently enacted ordinance, or if the use was once valid under the zoning ordinance, but the zoning ordinance was subsequently modified.

The importance of identifying such nonconforming use is that many ordinances prohibit the expansion or intensification in use of a nonconforming property. Similarly, it is also important to determine conformance of the structure with the area and dimensional requirements of the ordinances. For example, current zoning may require twenty-foot side yard setbacks, but the structure was built before the requirement was imposed, and it has only ten-foot side yard setbacks. Again, the importance here is that while the structure may be used for its current purposes, because it is dimensionally nonconforming, many zoning ordinances prohibit the expansion of the structure. By way of example, if the required side yard setback is twenty feet, and the structure is set back ten feet on one side and thirty feet on the other side, the ordinance may prohibit expansion of the conforming side of the structure to come within twenty feet of the side yard, which would normally be permissible, but is impermissible because the other side is nonconforming. Ordinances vary on this issue, so specific research is required.

Other zoning issues may include an examination of variances, deviations, and special exceptions of record that may pertain to the property and limit its use, or an examination of the scope of such relief if that is necessary for proposed development or redevelopment. Are there outstanding notices of violation? Is the lot a valid subdivided lot of record, and what restrictions of record apply? Are there cultural, religious, or archeological requirements or restrictions of record? Are there historic district requirements and restrictions, or overlay district requirements or restrictions? A number of communities in Rhode Island have local historic district requirements that apply to coastal properties and may significantly limit new construction, redesign, or reconstruction of the properties. Wickford, a historic waterfront village in North Kingstown, and East Greenwich's Hill and Harbor District are examples. I am aware of property owners in one town who spent two years trying to get approval for significant expansion of their waterfront historic structure before finally abandoning the effort.

When evaluating the physical property and land use restrictions, consider requiring an architect, engineer, or surveyor to complete a zoning report indicating current zoning requirements, including maximum height, minimum area, lot coverage ratios, setbacks, open space, parking, etc., and comparing that with existing property information for the property in question. The report could include a required zoning certificate from the building or zoning official, as is the custom in the particular municipality.

Structure
A detailed physical inspection of the property is a standard due diligence item, including structural, HVAC (heating, ventilating, and air conditioning), electrical, mechanical, and plumbing. Is there deferred maintenance? If extensive, the cost of correction can be high. You can also request that the inspector review municipal records to see if there are any violations of record. For example, in addition to the issues pertaining to structures nonconforming as to dimension as discussed above, consider also municipal record review to determine whether there are any notices of violation

issued for building, fire, or life safety code matters. Are there any warranties or guarantees pertaining to the structure, including warranty bonds, or existing maintenance contracts that may be assigned? Such warranties may also give a purchaser claims for prior work not done properly.

With regard to the structure, one set of questions is whether it meets current requirements. The answer may be that in fact it does because of grandfathering. In other words, it may meet CRMC requirements for setback from the coastal feature because the structure predated the requirements and was grandfathered. Or it may meet building code requirements because it was built before building codes were in existence or was built to a less protective building code standard that was applicable at the time of the construction.

But that may not be the end of the inquiry for a prudent purchaser. For example, it may be beneficial to ask whether the structure meets current CRMC setback standards. If not, and it is substantially destroyed, it will be necessary to relocate the structure in order to reconstruct it, such that it is in compliance with current setback requirements. This may not be desirable or feasible given the lot size and configuration. Similarly, it may be asked whether it would meet current building code requirements. If not, the structure may be vulnerable in the event of a severe storm. The CRMC Coastal Guide, on page 21, presents questions to ask in this regard and ways to determine the answers. For instance, inspection by a qualified engineer may be appropriate. And if a structure that does not meet current building codes was substantially destroyed, it would have to be rebuilt to current building code standards, which could include, *inter alia*, elevating the structure to ensure living quarters are above base flood elevation.

Even if the structure would not meet current CRMC setback requirements or current building code requirements, the decision may nevertheless be to purchase it. That decision will, however, be a fully informed decision.

Survey and Title

A survey is often not considered when a completed dwelling is being purchased, particularly if there are no plans to expand the structure or to construct outbuildings, etc. However, a survey can reveal encroachments, such as a neighboring driveway extending over the property line, or a structure nonconforming with all dimensional requirements. A survey can also locate easements on the property that may have been identified in a title search. Purchasers of waterfront property should particularly consider getting a survey, and ensure that the surveyor includes the mean high tide line as established by the eighteen-year Metonic cycle, as this is capable of arithmetic determination and sets the boundary between private property and state public trust land, where applicable. (The boundary between private property at the shore and public property is discussed in more detail in chapter 6.) And where rights of way or other easements may be implicated, as rights of third parties to access the water through the property being purchased, a survey may be particularly important.

The title search itself is a critical component of due diligence, and any lender financing a purchase will require that the purchaser cause a lender's title insurance policy to be issued to the lender. This will confirm ownership of the property, reveal liens or mortgages of record that must be discharged, provide the legal description of the property, identify easements of record, and otherwise address the status of title to the property. It is often mistakenly believed that the longer a title has been held by the current owner, the cleaner it will be; or if the abutting properties are owned by family members, the less title problems there will be. In my experience, this is not necessarily the case. The longer title has been held, the less it has been examined and the less opportunity there has been to identify and correct problems. A property that sells every five years on the average may well present fewer title issues that a property held in the same ownership for seventy years. Similarly, when family members own abutting properties, they sometimes do things improperly that cloud title, as they may not exercise the same formalities in dealing with family as they would do in dealing with strangers.

Regarding the title insurance policy, discuss with your attorney the potential benefits of getting endorsements for such matters as zoning, access, contiguous parcels, etc. While these increase the cost of the title insurance premium, they are a way of doing due diligence that also provides the benefits of insurance.

Utilities

If the property is undeveloped, are all required utilities run to the perimeter of the property, or must some lines be extended? If so, at whose cost and on what timeline? If the property is developed, are all required utilities available at the perimeter? For example, is a natural gas line available in the event you are contemplating converting the heating system from oil to gas? Is the capacity of the utilities adequate? This could be a critical issue if the property is being acquired for development or change of use. Is the property served by a combined sewer overflow? If so, are there requirements to install new sewer lines because the regulator is preventing any connection to CSOs in the area? Such new installation requirements would likely pertain only to new construction, but they can add significantly to the cost of a project.

Two other major utility issues pertaining to coastal properties in Rhode Island are important to consider. The first pertains to onsite sewage systems. Many properties in proximity to the coast in Rhode Island are not serviced by municipal sewers, but rather by on-site disposal systems. In Rhode Island, unlike Massachusetts, there is no governmental requirement that these systems be inspected and certified as functioning as a part of the real estate sales process. Accordingly, take care to know what you are getting.

If the property is serviced by a cesspool, be aware that the Rhode Island General Assembly passed legislation in 2007 (RI Gen. Laws 23–19.15–1 *et seq.*) ordering the phase out of thousands of cesspools based on the finding that they are substandard for sewage treatment and disposal, contribute directly to groundwater and surface water contamination, and discharge bacteria, viruses, and other pollutants.

The legislation would eliminate cesspools that have failed, are on property where sewer connection is available at the property line, are within two hundred feet of a public water well or surface water supply, or are within two hundred feet of the inland edge of a shoreline feature bordering tidal water. Cesspools serving a multifamily dwelling or non-residential facility must also be replaced. Of the estimated fifty thousand cesspools in Rhode Island, approximately four thousand are estimated to be in the state's coastal zone.

Under the original legislation, failed cesspools had to be removed within one year of discovery or sooner if an imminent health hazard was posed. Cesspools on property with a sewer stub had to be replaced within one year of sale of the property, and cesspools within two hundred feet of tidal coastal features or a water supply had to be replaced by January 1, 2013. The deadlines could be extended up to five years for demonstrated undue hardship.

This generated a good bit of controversy, and the legislative deadlines have been extended.

As of July 8, 2014, the DEM listed the following deadlines for certain cesspools:

1. All cesspools within the two hundred-foot zones identified above will have to be inspected upon notice from DEM and no later than January 1, 2012;
2. All cesspools within the two hundred-foot zones identified above that are found to be failed will need to be replaced within one year of discovery;
3. All cesspools within the two hundred-foot zones identified above that are found in already sewered areas will need to be hooked up to the sewer no later than January 1, 2014; and
4. All other cesspools within the two hundred-foot zones identified above will need to be replaced by January 1, 2014.

Again, such deadlines can be extended for up to five years for demonstrated undue hardship.

While this book was being written, the Rhode Island General Assembly passed legislation signed by the governor, to be effective January 1, 2016, which amends this statutory structure and requires that upon the sale of property served by a cesspool in the sensitive areas described above, the building must be connected to a sewer if a sewer stub is available, or if not available, to an approved on-site wastewater treatment system; in either event the new connection must be made not later than twelve months following the date of sale. Certain transfers of property are exempted, as for example, transfers among family members or certain transfers to trusts. The thought was that the cost of the connection to a new system is something that could be accommodated in the price negotiations for the property at the time of sale, perhaps easing the financial burden of making the switchover.

Also, do not fail to check municipal requirements if there is a cesspool on the property at issue, as many municipalities have established their own requirements for phase out of cesspools. For example, in South Kingstown, cesspools must be phased out and replaced with an onsite wastewater system either five years from its first inspection or within twelve months of the property's sale, whichever is sooner (S.K. Ordinance 19–157[9]). As noted in chapter 6, I think there is a real question whether many of the local ordinance addressing environmental issues regulated by the state are invalid under the restrictions on the scope of home rule by municipalities under our state constitution and applicable case law. Unfortunately, a resolution of such unenforceability will generally require litigation, although as further discussed in chapter 6, a state task force recommended legislation in this area pertaining to wetlands and individual sewage disposal systems, which was passed by the General Assembly while this book was being written.

If you are buying a coastal property with a cesspool, even if it is not within the sensitive areas described above and therefore not requiring replacement within a year of the transfer, during your due diligence you should consider that requirements for removal may be imposed, and you should expect to be required to ultimately remove the system. If sewers are not available, and your property is close to sensitive water bodies, or has water table issues, talk with an engineer. You may need an advanced wastewater treatment system, which at approximately thirty thousand dollars or more installed could cost twice the cost of a standard ISDS system.

The second issue to consider with regard to utilities in coastal Rhode Island is whether water supply is adequate. This most often tends to arise when the source of water supply is individual wells as opposed to municipal service. In some coastal areas, particularly those with an inundation of people in the summer months, water supply wells can be sorely taxed, with rationing sometimes necessary, and with wells sometimes running dry. In some areas, an association of homeowners may have their own well water distribution system, and in others it may be a case of individual wells, or a combination of both. However, given proximity to the coast, some wells can become tainted with brackish water, and given hydrogeological conditions, some wells may be inadequate for the demand presented. Accordingly, certainly when private wells are involved, your due diligence should address capacity, quality (i.e., are wells impacted by bacteria, salt water, etc.) and the operation, maintenance, management, and control of the supply system.

Permits and Registration

Required permits may range from certificates of occupancy, required for all occupied dwellings; permits for special exceptions, retail permits, elevator permits, boiler permits, sidewalk encroachment permits, and business permits, such as for a restaurant, entertainment, liquor license, outdoor entertainment, lodging, etc. Obviously, for acquisition of a business, permits may be an important focus of the due diligence inquiry. For coastal properties, some permits can be critical. If you are buying a structure with a dock, you will want to ensure that the dock is properly permitted by the CRMC. That permit may have been obtained to allow construction of the dock, or if the dock is grandfathered, having existed prior to the time the Coastal Resources Management Council was created in 1971. Depending on the type of water in which the dock is located (from Type 1, most sensitive, to Type 6, least protected), if the dock is not permitted and if it could not be installed under today's regulatory scheme—for example, new residential docks are not permitted in Type 1 waters—the dock must be removed. Recently, the CRMC successfully sued a marina to remove its docks in Type 1 waters, despite the fact the docks had been there for decades and served over forty boaters, since the marina operator could not demonstrate that it ever had a permit from the CRMC or the Army Corps of Engineers. It was an unpermitted facility, and it was required to cease and desist, and no new permit would be issued on existing regulations.

Accordingly, if you are buying a residence or marina with in-water facility, do not assume you will be able to use those facilities simply because they are there. Check with the CRMC to determine the type of water involved (Type 1 to Type 6) and whether any permit exists to allow the continued operation of the facilities.

With further regard to permits, the Rhode Island General Assembly had, beginning in November 2009, extended the normal expiration of certain permits required for development, including permits issued by the State Department of Environmental Management, the Coastal Resources Management Council, and municipal planning and zoning permits. The extensions were granted over the years because the economic downturn made it difficult to either get financing for development or, even if financing was not an issue, find a robust rental or sale market for the developed project. Under legislation signed by the governor in the summer of 2015, the suspension of the tolling period for these development permits expires July 1, 2016, when all of the tolled permits will start to run. Accordingly, someone buying coastal property dependent on development permits will want to verify with the issuing agency when the work under that permit must be undertaken to avoid seeking a new permit.

Tenancies

The coastal property being acquired may be an apartment complex, office building, or retail facility that perhaps depends, for its investment value, on its income-generating potential from tenants. Assuming a prospective purchaser has confirmed zoning, compliance with building codes, etc. as discussed above, appropriate due diligence may well also include a review of leases, certificates of occupancy for tenants, if applicable, rent rolls, amount of security deposits, etc. As a part of the lease review, a purchaser will also want to ensure that no tenants have a right of first offer or right of first refusal to buy the property, or if so, whether or not they have been waived. A prospective purchaser will also want to determine early termination rights of tenants, if any, or extension rights at rental rates unfavorable to the property owner, or expansion rights that could impact a purchaser's plans, or limitations on tenants to whom a new owner could rent, etc. A prospective purchaser would also be advised to require estoppel certificates from existing tenant to ensure they are not claiming the landlord is in breach of their lease, there is confirmation of the amount of the security deposit being held, there are no claimed defects of the property, there are no claims against the landlord, etc. Any such claims could be inherited by a new purchaser.

Insurance

If the property at issue is unique for its structure, a prospective purchaser may want to consider obtaining a certificate of insurance, as discussed in chapter 3, to be assured that coverage is sufficient for reconstruction (and, of course, a purchaser will want to ensure that reconstruction is not prohibited by applicable law because the property is in a sensitive or regulated location). Also, if the property at issue is unique for its location, but not its structure, and/or if the removal of the structure is planned, a purchaser may want to ensure that in the event of destruction, the seller's policy covers debris removal costs.

One major issue for due diligence inquiry is the determination as to whether the property is in a flood hazard area and whether it requires flood insurance. This issue is a primary concern to lenders, who will not make a loan to a property requiring flood insurance without the buyer/owner having that flood insurance in place. This is discussed in depth in chapter 5, dealing with financing issues. Given the importance of this issue to lenders, all purchasers of property in a flood hazard area (including those who may be buying with cash and will not have a conventional mortgage) should understand the flood insurance issue and should consider the advisability of purchasing flood insurance. While buyers of substantial means could certainly come to the conclusion that given the cost of flood insurance, and their determination of how likely it is that a substantial flood may damage their property, self-insurance is a reasonable alternative, that is, in any event, a process that should be investigated and determined, not ignored.

Not only should flood insurance be on a buyer's list of due diligence issues, even if financing is not being sought to fund the purchase, it should also be considered with regard to timing factors under the purchase and sale agreement in the event that financing is being sought. For example, assume a buyer has forty days to conduct due diligence activities, but only twenty days under the mortgage contingency clause. The buyer therefore has twenty days under his mortgage contingency clause, at which time the buyer must either have a mortgage commitment, whereupon he waives the mortgage contingency clause, or terminate the transaction for failure to qualify for financing. Assume the buyer receives commitment, thereby waiving the mortgage contingency clause, and later during the forty-day due diligence inspections determines that the property is in a flood hazard area and flood insurance must be procured. The cost of that flood insurance, under new legislative rules, could be so costly that the buyer would no longer qualify for its financing. Accordingly, the buyer would need to have a basis for terminating the transaction under the terms of its purchase and sale agreement or face default if the transaction could not close without financing. So while this is discussed in detail in the chapter on financing and closing the transaction, it is something that a prospective buyer should not only integrate into due diligence, but should address in conjunction with qualifying for financing.

Governance Structures

Oftentimes, a property being acquired will be governed by condominium documents, homeowner association restrictions, covenants, conditions, and restrictions of record (sometimes referred to in shorthand as CCRs), or the terms of a ground lease. In any event, review of these documents is a required part of due diligence, and their terms and conditions can have a material impact on the financial transaction or on the use of the property. With regard to condominiums, pay particular attention to these documents. Rhode Island has a comprehensive and thorough condominium act based on the model act, and it is not uncommon for condominium documents to be at odds with required provisions of the Rhode Island statute. It is also not unheard of for the documents to actually be defective. For example, I know of one instance where someone selected his condominium unit and purchased it, or at least thought he purchased it. Actually, he purchased another unit in the complex because the referenced plans differed from the recorded condominium declaration. I am also aware of an instance where a buyer purchased a condominium unit, but the plans were so defective, depending on what side of the bed he was sleeping on, he was either in or out of his unit (that is a slight exaggeration, but not much of one). By the way, that particular purchaser was a lawyer!

Miscellaneous

If an important part of the transaction is the assumption of existing contracts, whether management agreements, broker's agreements, employment agreements, or services, material, and maintenance agreements, you may well want to get estoppel certificates from the party contracting with the property owner to ensure there are no claimed breaches or defaults, no claims of money owed, or other liabilities impacting the validity of the contact or the property.

Also, while condemnation appears to be less rather than more frequent in recent years, it may be advisable to check with municipal offices to determine if there is any proposed condemnation, whether by the municipality or the state.

Finally, a prospective purchaser should pay attention to requirements his lender may establish as part of the financing commitment. This could encompass anything from financial documentation pertaining to the property or business operation being acquired, if it is primarily an investment transaction, to concerns about the environmental condition of the property, and perhaps at least a Phase I site assessment. Environmental issues are discussed in the following section.

Environmental Due Diligence Issues

Environmental due diligence is crucial because the consequences for missing a significant environmental condition on a property being acquired can range from serious to catastrophic. Many environmental laws impose a type of strict liability, oftentimes not requiring that a property owner even caused the environmental condition in order to be held completely responsible for its cleanup. For example, the primary federal hazardous materials statute, the Comprehensive Environmental Response, Compensation and Liability Act, 42 US C. 9601 *et. seq.* (familiarly known as CERCLA or the federal Superfund law), imposes strict, joint and several, and retroactive liability. Parties liable under CERCLA include:

- the current owner and/or operator of the property contaminated;
- the owner and/or operator of the property at the time of the release;
- anyone arranging for disposal of a substance that was subsequently released at another site; and
- anyone transporting a substance to a site from which it was subsequently released.

Under such a merciless liability scheme, the following individuals would be liable for the cost of environmental cleanup (unless the party qualified for, and successfully bore the burden of proving, one of several narrow defenses, including being an innocent landowner or a property owner whose property was impacted by a release from another site):

- A purchaser who bought the property without notice or knowledge it was contaminated.
- An owner who hired a licensed transporter to ship hazardous materials from its property to a licensed disposal site in conformance with all laws, and there was a subsequent release of hazardous materials from that site.
- A party who disposed of hazardous materials in conformance with all applicable laws *before* Congress passed CERCLA, but the disposed hazardous waste now constitutes a violation of CERCLA.
- A party who disposed of only 2 percent of the material at a disposal facility from which there was a release could be liable for the entire cleanup of that release.

Rhode Island has its own mini-CERCLA statute, the Industrial Property Remediation and Reuse Act, RI Gen. Laws 23–19.14–1 *et seq.*, which imposes a similar liability scheme under Rhode Island law.

Under such a liability scheme, the concept of "innocent" is indeed illusive. It is a liability scheme designed to ensnare as many people as possible in order to get as much money as possible for cleanup. This counsels caution for purchasers where environmental issues are involved, particularly in the context of hazardous wastes or hazardous materials.

After all, this is just one of the Rhode Island statutes that impose liability for violations of environmental laws. There are dozens of statutes and regulations in Rhode Island alone, under the jurisdiction of various regulators, which impose significant sanctions for violations of environmental laws. These violations can result not just in civil fines, but criminal prosecution as well, and fines can run as high as twenty-five thousand dollars per day, per violation. In fact, fines can be so onerous that just the threat of imposition of the fines can force someone to settle with the regulator rather than continue the fight.

The simple fact is that in acquiring real estate, you ignore environmental due diligence at your peril. Finding problems before the purchase transaction may derail the transaction, but not finding them until after the closing can be catastrophic. That being said, environmental professionals performing environmental due diligence will be the first to say they cannot guarantee that because they did not find a problem, one does not exist. In other words, there are no guarantees that even a quality environmental investigation will turn up every problem.

While many people think of coastal properties as pertaining to residential properties, it is not uncommon in Rhode Island to find commercial and even industrial properties in coastal areas. Accordingly, in addressing environmental due diligence, I will occasionally address those issues that may be peculiar to industrial or commercial properties.

Environmental Assessments
The most common form of environmental site assessments are the so-called Phase I Site Assessment and the Phase II Site Assessment, protocols for which have been developed by the American Society of Testing Materials and have been determined to meet the requirements of the All Appropriate Inquiries Rule promulgated by the Environmental Protection Agency (40 CFR Part 312), which became effective November 1, 2006. This rule established standards to determine whether a site assessment

was sufficiently extensive to allow the purchaser to claim the protections of certain limited defenses under CERCLA.

A Phase I Site Assessment would include a records review pertaining to the property to determine matters of importance to environmental concerns, a site inspection, and a listing of any recognized environmental conditions found on the site. Recognized environmental conditions means the existence or likely existence of hazardous substances, including petroleum, arising from a release or that threaten a release. The Phase I Site Assessment may or may not recommend a Phase II Site Assessment, which is a more detailed and thorough review of site conditions and specific recognized environmental conditions. A Phase II Site Assessment often involves intrusive testing, such as drilling and sampling of ground water and soil.

While meeting the requirements of the All Appropriate Inquiries Rule is helpful for claiming CERCLA defenses, those requirements do not encompass a number of environmental conditions that could materially impair the value of the property and potentially be very expensive to remove and/or remediate, including without limitation lead, PCBs, and mold. For that reason, simply relying on the scope of the All Appropriate Inquiries Rules is inadequate for most purchasers. Accordingly, purchasers will want to determine the scope of services of their consultant to inspect and test for other environmental conditions, many of which are set forth in this section. These could include inspections to determine whether a business operation on-site is in compliance with applicable regulatory rules, such as disposal of substances to a municipal sewer system or air emission requirements.

Scope of Environmental Inspections

In addition to the standard Phase I and Phase II Site Assessment to meet the requirements of CERCLA's All Appropriate Inquiries Rule, buyers should also entertain inspections for asbestos, wetlands, mold and indoor air quality, radon, Native American artifacts and cultural resources, lead, PCBs, urea formaldehyde, chlorofluorocarbons, underground storage tanks (and related piping), onsite disposal facilities, whether historic or existing (such as lagoons, pits, trenches, landfills, etc.), storm water collection and runoff facilities, notices of violations issued against the property, and releases or evidences of releases of hazardous materials on the property.

The environmental consultant is a key member of the due diligence team, and the contract with the consultant should reflect this. It should specifically define the scope of services to be provided and where appropriate, the key personnel who will provide the services. Pay attention to the indemnification provisions. Most form contracts will try to limit the liability of the consultant, often to damages that do not exceed the contract price. It is advisable to reject this, while an appropriate compromise may be to accept a limitation to the scope of insurance proceeds, as long as one is comfortable with the scope of the environmental consultant's insurance coverage and the coverage amounts (and one is comfortable that the policy maximum could not be overwhelmed by other claims against the consultant). Also, depending on the nature of the due diligence inquiry, it may be appropriate to negotiate a detailed environmental audit protocol that the consultant is required to follow. This ensures that the prospective purchaser will receive the most useful information in a format that is of most help in the particular transaction. This is particularly appropriate where the property being investigated may be an ongoing business enterprise, such as a manufacturing facility.

Existing Operations

With regard to properties involving ongoing business operations, whether commercial or industrial, it may well be important to identify hazardous waste generation and solid waste generation at the property. It may also be important to conduct an environmental compliance audit of existing operations, including storage, shipment, and disposal of hazardous materials. To the extent the facility has pollution treatment, pretreatment, or control facilities, these will require inspection as well. Sometimes the specialized nature of the business or operations being inspected will narrow the environmental consulting firms from which a purchaser can chose, as some firms simply may not have the expertise the purchaser requires.

Environmental Permits

Environmental permits are often of particular importance to ongoing business operations. Qualified environmental consultants can inspect a facility, determine what permits are required to be issued, confirm their issuance, and determine that they have not expired and that there are no open notices of violations for the activities for which the permits are issued. If permits must be transferred to a new owner, this should also be identified.

However, environmental permits may also be of importance to residential properties. For example, if there is an underground storage tank for fuel oil of a size regulated by the Department of Environmental Management (i.e., 1,100 gallons or larger), there should be a permit on file with the DEM for the tank, and the permit should be transferred at the time of conveyance of the property. While the line between real estate and environmental permits may sometimes be blurry, Assents (which are in fact permits) issued by the Coastal Resources Management Council are often important in the residential context. For instance, if there is a dock at the property being acquired, is there an Assent on file permitting that dock? If the answer is no, and the dock is in Type 1 waters, it may be unauthorized. If so, it may have to be removed, and a new dock may not be allowed.

Wetlands and On-site/Proximate Conditions

This is one of the most important areas of inquiry of the due diligence investigation, as these are matters that either directly touch and burden the property, or are in such close proximity to the property that they could have a material impact on the property. One of the most important for purposes of coastal properties is wetlands. Wetlands can render a property essentially unbuildable, or at least not capable of supporting what a purchaser wants to build on the property. Consider the example given in the opening pages of this chapter, where wetlands precluded building on most of the property in question, and ultimately, after a protracted application and hearing procedure, and recourse to the courts to overturn the agency's refusal to issue the permit, all that was allowed on a multi-acre lot was a tiny house footprint, no garage, no recreation area, and with most of the property dedicated to a protective easement.

Unfortunately for purchasers, it takes an experienced professional to identify wetlands, as land that appears to be dry may in fact be wet, as identified by vegetation and subsurface conditions. An experienced wetlands biologist can walk a site, flag wetlands, and advise as to what a regulator may or may not allow to be done on the impacted portions of the site.

In addition to wetlands, which may include streams, ponds, or rivers, the presence of tidal water bodies on the property can significantly impact what type of development CRMC will allow or prohibit. This is discussed in detail in chapter 6.

In the due diligence inquiry, a prospective purchaser should also carefully consider conditions in proximity to the property, such as dams, water retention/detention facilities, waste disposal sites, releases of hazardous materials, raw material storage areas, waste or fuel storage areas, and motor vehicle maintenance and repair areas. Sometimes, what is off-site may be more important than what is on-site. I once saw a residential property that was adjacent to a former municipal garage, which was subsequently used as a storage area for salt for winter ice control purposes. It turns out that waste oil from the former garage had impacted the adjacent residential property, and the new use of the site, salt storage, also resulted in contamination of the ground water on the residential property. Now, that was *not* a good neighbor.

Additionally, even in Rhode Island, which recognizes an "innocent down-site receptor" as not being responsible for removal or remediation of contamination emanating from off-site, the impact of the contamination could nevertheless make the property unsuitable for the purchaser's purposes, and it could well preclude obtaining a loan to acquire the property. It is therefore prudent to pay careful attention to what is in proximity to the property you want to acquire.

Water Supply

Private water supply systems serving multiple properties are generally regulated, requiring permits from the Rhode Island Department of Health, and in coastal communities it is not uncommon to see a local association of homeowners operate wells to supply potable water to the residents of the area. Even if a permit is in place, as discussed above, it may be important to confirm the overall capacity of the system. In some areas with a low wintertime population but a high summertime population, water can run out toward the end of the summer. Moreover, private potable water supply wells should be tested during the due diligence process, as testing is required by Rhode Island Department of Health Regulations prior to sale of the property (Rules and Regulations Pertaining to Private Drinking Water Systems, Rule 11.1(b) [June 2008]). Note also that private wells must be disclosed, as well as any known contamination, by the seller and that the water testing is to be done at the buyer's expense (RI Gen. Laws 5–20.8–12). Failure of the seller to make necessary disclosures or failure to provide previous well water test results allows the buyer to void the transaction at closing (RI Gen. Laws 5–20.8–12). Further information about such testing can be obtained from the Rhode Island Department of Health's website. Additionally, if the site is undeveloped and a structure is proposed, the Department of Health must verify acceptable water quality, and once verified, the municipality may issue a permit for the well. However, if the development project is for multiple family use, with a well serving over fifteen people, it is no longer considered a private well, and the Department of Health may no longer have jurisdiction, under regulations that were being drafted as this book was written. Additionally, regulation of the drilling of the well falls under the Rhode Island Contracting Board, although a variance may involve application to other agencies, such as the DEM for wetlands issues, or the municipality regarding variances for setbacks from local roads.

Information from the Seller

Often, an important source of environmental due diligence is the seller itself. This is particularly the case when the sale involves an ongoing business operation—unlike in a residential transaction, the seller may well be anticipating having to provide certain environmental information. For example, in sophisticated commercial transactions, it is not uncommon to require in the purchase and sale agreement that the seller respond to an environmental questionnaire that may be attached as an exhibit to the agreement. It is also not uncommon to seek warranties and representations from the seller on environmental issues. And even the process of negotiating the agreement can be part of the due diligence process, as often what the seller refuses to certify to or warrant and represent may be identified as prime areas of inquiry.

To the extent the seller has done his own environmental site assessments or self-audits, these can be requested, as can other environmental testing or reports done for the benefit of the seller.

Rhode Island has enacted what is called the Rhode Island Environmental Compliance Incentive Act (RI Gen. Laws 42–17.8, *et seq.*) to promote self-monitoring of certain regulated environmentally impactful activities of regulated businesses or persons who conduct regulated activities. The Act defines an environmental audit as a "systematic, documented and objective review of a regulated entity's facility operations and occupational practices which affect the regulated entity's compliance with environmental laws." *Id.* § 42–17.8–2(e). These entities may self-audit by hiring an environmental professional to assess the compliance of the facility with environmental requirements, any violations thereof, and the gravity of the environmental infraction. This report will then be further assessed by additional environmental experts. Communications regarding a potentially self-assessed violation remain confidential, and so long as the violating entity follows the Act's reporting guidelines, the violations cannot be reported to the attorney general or any other agency for civil or criminal prosecution. Violations may be remedied or mitigated within sixty days of being reported to the DEM, which may then either forgive the violation entirely or require a written consent order requiring the violator to maintain compliance with the environmental laws.

To the extent the proposed acquisition of a coastal property involves a business, a prospective purchaser can always request any such self-audit, though there is no obligation of the seller to provide the self-audits.

A purchaser would also want to inquire of the seller as to pending or threatened litigation, delivery of notices from private parties pertaining to issues that could lead to claims or litigation, and delivery of notices of violations or inquiries from the government pertaining to environmental matters.

Finally, in a transaction where a seller refuses to cooperate and be forthcoming with information about its property, even when appropriate confidentiality agreements are offered, a purchaser may want to reconsider the advisability of proceeding with the acquisition.

CHAPTER 5

FINANCING AND CLOSING THE TRANSACTION

While buying the property is obviously of great importance, as is ensuring you have sufficient funds to close the transaction, if the purchaser has followed the suggestions set forth in the prior chapters, the closing of the transaction should be somewhat anticlimactic, and hopefully largely uneventful. The brevity of this chapter reflects that.

In order to make it uneventful, it is important that you, and as to some matters perhaps, your legal counsel, have done everything to anticipate and address concerns or questions your lender may have, so that issues do not arise just before closing or at the closing table that literally call into question whether or not the loan will close. And it is important that your legal counsel has addressed purchase issues with the seller's counsel well in advance of the closing, such that the closing is a relatively quick and orderly process. I have represented buyers and sellers in complicated commercial transactions involving tens of millions of dollars, multitenant properties, and major construction projects that have closed in a couple of hours, with no surprises, no shouting, no questions that lacked answers, and no histrionics. Yet, I have seen some residential closings encounter all of those problems at the closing, simply because one or both lawyers had not prepared properly. This brief chapter will address how to make sure the financing and the closing both go smoothly.

Financing

A lender is going to have three primary concerns. The first is the credit-worthiness of the borrower. Can the purchaser afford the property; can he or she repay the loan? The second is the value of the property. Does it properly appraise such that the lender is satisfied with the loan to value ratio? The third is the conditions of the property not reflected in the appraisal. Are there title issues, environmental conditions, zoning or subdivision issues, or regulatory issues that impact the ability to build on the property, or expand it, if that is the plan, or the ability to use the property for its intended purpose? Within this third category falls an issue that looms large for lenders when coastal properties are being financed, as a result of recent federal legislative changes, and that is the necessity of flood insurance and its cost if it is required.

As to the first issue, the creditworthiness of the borrower, that is between the borrower and its lender, and there is not much legal counsel can do to address that issue. The second issue is largely between the lender and the appraiser, although the purchaser and/or his legal counsel may be in a position to provide information to the appraiser to address questions or concerns he may have or to help him understand facts pertaining to the structure of the transaction, etc. This is often important in complex commercial transactions or residential transactions with complicating factors.

It is on the third issue, conditions pertaining to the property, where the purchaser and his lawyer and other advisors and consultants may be particularly helpful.

Title Issues

For example, with regard to title, I recommend this be addressed early in the process, as a thorough title examination may reveal significant issues impacting the value of the property, its current use, or its intended use. For that reason, it is advisable to have a title examination commenced as soon as the purchase and sale agreement is signed. The Rhode Island Association of Realtors forms do not address this. If there are title issues, it may take time to address them and cure any defects. For example, I was once involved in a situation pertaining to the sale of a significant coastal property where skilled title counsel identified title issues arising from trustee conveyances following the death of one of the owners. Curing the issue involved the drafting and preparation of memoranda of trusts and deeds involving two different trusts, including out-of-state trustees, which took several weeks to resolve. While everyone was committed to favorable resolution, that nevertheless took time.

In considering title issues, also consider endorsements to the title insurance policy that the purchaser or the lender may want in order to further protect the owner's or lender's interests and to facilitate the loan closing. These may include a zoning endorsement ensuring that the use of the property complies with zoning, a contiguous parcels endorsement if there is more than one parcel being purchased, or a restrictions and encroachments endorsements to ensure there are no covenants, conditions, or restrictions that could divest the lien of the lender's mortgage.

And if title problems are encountered, it is important that the purchaser and counsel never present a title problem to a lender without also presenting a solution, because only a solution will result in the lender making the loan and funding the acquisition.

As indicated previously, one issue that lenders will focus on is recent changes in federal law pertaining to flood insurance, which has resulted in steep cost increases for insurance and created turmoil in the coastal properties market. For that reason, this issue will be addressed in depth. While it is addressed here under financing issues, this is because lenders require a property owner to carry flood insurance in a flood hazard area and not because if a purchaser is not using a lender, flood insurance should not be an issue. Purchasers who may be buying coastal properties with cash without benefit of a lender should also be looking at flood insurance if they are buying in a flood hazard area, as noted in chapter 4, discussing due diligence issues.

Flood Insurance Rate Increases

Recent changes in federal law have dramatically changed the flood insurance program, with one of the primary foci being to eliminate subsidized premium rates for flood insurance, so that rates would be allowed to rise to actuarially sound levels—meaning that the rate structure fairly compensates the insurers for the true risk of flooding of the property. When these changes were put into effect by federal legislation, there was a dramatic increase in flood insurance premiums for many properties, and a resultant outcry from homeowners, investors, and realtors that the changes made some properties unaffordable and unsalable. Given that this situation is still evolving as this book is being written, some further background will be very helpful to you in understanding how things have changed and what further changes may be in the offing.

It has been estimated that 90 percent of all natural disasters involve flooding, and flooding in the United States is frequent and widespread.

Congress created the National Flood Insurance Program in 1968, responding to the reality that as a result of flooding along the Mississippi River in the 1960s, flood insurance was virtually unattainable in the private insurance market, according to the National Association of Insurance Commissioners. In addition to providing flood insurance, the program administered by the Federal Emergency Management Agency (FEMA) also developed maps of flood hazard zones.

Flood zones are designated based on the risk of flooding in the zone. As the CRMC Coastal Guide summarizes on page 8, a base flood is one that has approximately a 1 percent chance of occurring in any year, or once in one hundred years. Such zones would be expected to impact Special Flood Hazard Area zones A and V. Another categorization is if a flood would be expected to occur in two out of one thousand storms (or one out of five hundred storms), known as a five hundred-year storm, and such an area would be labeled as a 0.2 percent zone (i.e., 0.2 percent annual chance flood). As the CRMC Coastal Guide notes, if the property is not located in a flood zone, FEMA maps can also indicate if it is in a risk area and may in the future be in a flood zone, given, for example, sea level rise.

Under the program, property owners in communities that participate in regulatory programs to reduce flood damage can purchase flood insurance under the National Flood Insurance Program. Preexisting homes and businesses at the time of the program's adoption could remain in their then-current condition and could purchase flood insurance. For properties in certain high-risk flood areas, the rates did not reflect the true flood risk of the properties. The net result was that flooding of these "grandfathered"

high-risk properties resulted in payouts that undermined the financial sta-
bility of the National Flood Insurance Program (FEMA has said that only 20
percent of the properties in the NFIP received subsidized rates).

To qualify as a grandfathered property, the property must be located too low in the flood zone (i.e., below the base flood elevation)
through no fault of the owners. To meet this qualification for grandfathering, a property could fall into two primary categories. First, the
property structure must have been built before 1975 or before the community received its first Flood Insurance Rate Map (FIRM). Effectively,
to meet this requirement, at the time of the construction the structure
was not being built in an area already found to be a flood hazard area.
Alternatively, the property structure could have been built after issuance
of the Flood Insurance Rate Map, but built in full compliance with the applicable Flood Insurance Rate Map, pursuant to valid municipal permits,
and subsequent Flood Insurance Rate Maps show it in the flood zone at
greater risk of flooding. In other words, the construction was appropriate
in accordance with the existing FIRM, but the maps were changed after
the completion of construction.

Given the financial losses caused by flooding, particularly of grandfathered properties in high-risk areas where the premiums paid for the insurance did not reflect the true risk of flooding, Congress determined that
reform of the program was necessary. On July 6, 2012, President Obama
signed the Biggert-Waters Flood Insurance Reform Act of 2012. One of
the goals of the reform was to raise premium rates to reflect the actual
risk of a property flooding. As a result, some property owners in low-risk
areas actually saw reductions in premiums and other owners in high-risk
areas saw increases in rates, sometime dramatic increases. The Reform
Act also provided for the phase-out of the previously grandfathered and
subsidized policies by October and November 2013.

Under the 2012 reform law, primary residences in a Special Flood
Hazard Area were allowed to keep their subsidized rates unless or until
(i) the property is sold (ii) the policy lapses (iii) the property suffers severe,
repeated, flood losses or (iv) a new policy is purchased. However, those
with subsidized rates on nonprimary residences, such as a vacation house,
or on business property, would see 25 percent annual increases in rates
until actuarially sound rates were achieved.

The National Association of Counties reported examples of dramatic increases in rates when the Reform Act phases out grandfathering. One example was for a primary residence in Belle Chasse, Louisiana, which was built to code and never flooded, and would face an annual insurance premium increase from $632 to $17,723. In another example, a primary residence in Saint Petersburg Beach, Florida, built before FEMA issued flood maps (pre-FIRM) and never flooded, would see annual premiums go from $1,000 per year to $10,872 per year. A Rhode Island Emergency Management Agency official was quoted in the press as saying that the agency received reports of flood insurance policy increases in the tens of thousands of dollars and heard of one annual policy premium of $61,000- or approximately just over $5,000 per month.

These types of rate increases got property owners' attention, and they got Congress's attention. Congress reformed the Flood Insurance Reform Act in a stunning reversal in less than two years, which is breakneck speed for Congress.

On March 21, 2014, the president signed the Homeowner Flood Insurance Affordability Act of 2014 into law. That statute essentially undid some of the rate increases of the 2012 reform, including repealing rate increases already in effect and providing for refunds to certain policyholders who paid those increases.

The reform of the reform provides, with some exceptions, that primary residences (i.e., not vacation rentals or businesses) that were grandfathered will see premium increases of not less than 5 percent per annum and not more than 18 percent per annum until full actuarial rates are achieved, thereby preventing dramatic spikes in rates while moving toward actuarially sound rates. However, secondary residences and businesses are still subject to a 25 percent per year increase in premiums until actuarially sound rates are reached, as are severe repetitive loss properties receiving subsidized rates and buildings built before the FIRM that have been substantially damaged or improved.

The new legislation is setting forth what is clearly a work in progress, and there will likely be new issues, new requirements, and new regulations emerging as the new program is implemented.

But there is still more intrigue for Rhode Islanders on the flood insurance issue, at least as I now write this chapter.

Potentially Faulty FEMA Flood Maps

FEMA has issued new flood maps, and the new FEMA flood maps are certainly not without controversy and problems, at least here in New England.

This problem has been playing out quietly behind the scenes as I write this, but it will inevitably become very public, and it is something that all those purchasing, owning, or selling coastal properties should know about and be prepared for, because it could have a major impact on your property value.

FEMA has redone the maps for the East Coast up to New York using new technology and current assumptions and data. However, for whatever reason, in New England, through its regional office, it has used older technology and a forty-year-old methodology for calculating flood risks in areas, one that is not recommended for open ocean analysis, according to the executive director of the Rhode Island Coastal Resources Management Council.

According to my sources, the net result is that the maps for New England, including Rhode Island, underestimate the threat of flooding in open ocean areas and overestimate the threat of flooding in bay and inland areas. Looking at Rhode Island, I am told that the FEMA map calculations show flood levels in south county Rhode Island, along the south coast, at three to four feet *below* base flood elevation. As of this writing, there has not been enough work to determine how much it overstates the flood elevation levels in the bay areas, such as Greenwich Bay. (Base flood elevation, or BFE, is the 1 percent annual-chance flood, familiarly referred to as the hundred-year flood. BFE represents the elevation of the water during the base flood.)

The potential problems are significant and serious. For example, assume someone accepts the FEMA BFE level for a property fronting on the ocean and builds a new house to that standard. If FEMA later redraws the map, using newer technologies and methodologies, the base flood elevation for that property could increase by several feet, and the flood insurance premiums for the owners of that house could skyrocket. Yet, they relied on FEMA. Are we in need of more corrective legislation?

I am also told by Rhode Island's coastal regulator that the new FEMA New England maps use reduced data points along the shore, and that this, in combination with using the older calculation methodology, causes further distortion in the data and further inaccuracies in the true flood levels.

Rhode Island has met this head on, but other New England states have not yet geared up. First, Rhode Island told FEMA that FEMA was required to make a federal consistency filing under the Coastal Zone Management Act, because Rhode Island's coastal management plan lists changes in FEMA maps as an item that triggers a consistency filing under Rhode Island's Coastal Management Program. Apparently, not all other New England states have listed this as a trigger point under their coastal management programs. Under the Coastal Zone Management Act, certain activities requiring federal permits and certain activities by the federal government that could affect a state's coastal zone are required to be consistent with the enforceable policies of the state's coastal zone management plan.

After approximately one year, FEMA responded that its new maps were consistent with the enforceable policies of Rhode Island's coastal zone management program. Rhode Island disagrees with this consistency filing and is going to challenge it.

Moreover, Rhode Island has moved proactively by telling FEMA that it wants maps that accurately portray the actual risk of flooding. Rhode Island has offered to pay for its own mapping, and at this juncture I assume that is the way this controversy will get resolved, at least for Rhode Island.

But the critical thing for the rest of New England is to make a similar determination as to whether the New England FEMA maps distort flood risk.

This is, of course, not the end of the issue for those buying, owning, or selling coastal properties. It is certainly possible that, assuming the FEMA maps are redrawn, the new maps will increase the properties subject to flood hazard areas, thus requiring flood insurance for properties that may not have previously been required to procure insurance. In such an event it could be expected that there may be public outcry in these areas, because it will again raise premiums for properties exposed to the open ocean.

What should someone considering purchasing a coastal property do? The answer for now is pay attention, do your due diligence, determine what the current designation of the property at issue is, and stay tuned. This issue is likely to go through further changes as a result of new maps and perhaps further legislative or regulatory changes.

Also, be aware that there are non-FEMA options for flood insurance, such as insurance written through the Cat Coverage program, insured by a Lloyds of London affiliate, which can be discussed with an insurance agent specializing in flood insurance programs.

PART 2

Owning Coastal Property

P art II orients you to the realities of owning coastal property in Rhode Island, and at the center of that reality is regulatory jurisdiction, both at the state level and the municipal level. As noted frequently in this book, coastal property is some of the most heavily regulated property in the state of Rhode Island. Chapter 6 addresses this regulatory jurisdiction in the way coastal property owners are most often introduced to it—when they attempt to alter or improve their properties. The specific conditions that trigger such regulatory jurisdiction are discussed, and many are subtle and may in fact require an expert to identify. The conflicting nature of many of these regulations are also noted, although there is good news for property owners, given that the Rhode Island General Assembly has recently passed legislation to eliminate some of the conflicting and overlapping regulations pertaining to wetlands on onsite wastewater disposal systems. Chapter 7 addresses property boundary issues, as it is often not an easy determination as to where private property rights end and state access and other rights begin. This chapter includes a discussion of shore access issues and easement rights at the shore, as these have been an increasing source of conflict between private property owners and the public in recent years. Finally, chapter 8 addresses the issue of real estate taxation, as coastal properties are valuable and real estate taxes against them can be high. The steps for taxpayers to protect their challenge and appeal rights, at both the local and state level, can be difficult to understand and easily lost.

CHAPTER 6

RENOVATING EXISTING STRUCTURES AND NEW CONSTRUCTION

I n my experience, most buyers of already improved coastal property have plans to make further improvements, either by renovating existing structures, adding new structures to the property, such as a garage, or even taking down the existing structure and building a new one. Of course, if the property is vacant land, it is usually purchased for the purpose of constructing a new residence or some type of business structure. Indeed, I seldom see anyone buying waterfront property with plans to only paint, touch up, and move in.

Assuming the coastal property at issue is waterfront or very close to the water, virtually any alteration of an existing structure—a yard or outside area of the property, or any alteration of the shoreline feature—could (and often does) require regulatory approval, perhaps from several different regulators. And that is especially true of new construction.

If you own waterfront property in Rhode Island and think you can do with it what you will so long as you observe zoning ordinances like everyone else, you would be mistaken.

Coastal waterfront property in Rhode Island is heavily regulated by the Coastal Resources Management Council (CRMC) under a complex set of regulations found in the Rhode Island Coastal Resources Management Program. You ignore that regulatory structure at your peril.

It is also regulated by other state agencies, such as the Department of Environmental Management and the Department of Health, as discussed in chapter 2. Municipal regulations, even those outside of the scope of zoning ordinances, often apply, and as will be discussed below, sometimes conflict with state regulations.

By way of example, some years back one of my former law partners came to me with a problem—he had been served with a violation and penalty from the CRMC for "improving" his water view by removing some phragmites and other vegetation. CRMC had cited him for unauthorized alteration of a coastal wetland. Could I help, he asked?

After ascertaining more of the facts, I said he had a problem, but at least he hadn't hired a bulldozer to tear up the coastline. There was a long pause, and then he said, "Well, I did rent a Bobcat."

I said I could probably keep his wife out of jail, but he had better pack his toothbrush!

Of course, no one went to jail, but he did pay a fine, and the last I heard CRMC was discussing restoration of wetlands with him. Now, if a lawyer who should know better can get himself into this kind of problem, you can imagine what else may be going on along our coastline and the difficulties other waterfront property owners can get into if they are not aware of the regulations or do not follow them.

And lest you think I am exaggerating the potential complexity of altering coastal properties in Rhode Island: as I write this, there is an article on my desk from yesterday's *Wall Street Journal* entitled, "The Tough Road to a Waterfront House," which recounts the odyssey of a property owner to expand a nine-hundred-square-foot ranch house to a thirty-two-hundred-square-foot modern house on Rhode Island's Narragansett Bay, and his dealings with various state and municipal regulatory agencies. The process took six years! And the property owner was a lawyer! (The subheadline to the article is "A tenacious attorney spends years wrangling regulations to build on Rhode Island's Narragansett Bay.")

Even if you seek to comply with the regulations, you may not even be able to do what you want to do on the property. For example, if you had your heart set on installing a dock, and even have the boat ready to go into the water, if the property abuts Type 1 waters, the most protected coastal waters, you will not be installing a dock. Period. No permit or approval will issue from the CRMC, and judicial appeal will be fruitless.

And similar plans for improvements could meet similar fates, although depending on the improvements proposed, judicial appeals may be of some benefit even if permits are denied.

It is for this reason that due diligence is so strongly emphasized in chapter 4. You want to know before you buy that you can do with the property what you intend. Of course, plans change, families change, and circumstances change, and what was not even contemplated at purchase, such as building a guest house on the property, for example, is now a priority, and a new round of due diligence is necessary.

The purpose of this chapter is to provide a detailed overview of what is involved in the renovation of existing structures on the coast or the construction of a new structure. In doing so, I will occasionally refer to the CRMC Coastal Guide prepared for CRMC by the University of Rhode Island Coastal Resources Center/Rhode Island Sea Grant as a part of the Shoreline Change Special Area Management Plan (also known as the Beach Special Area Management Plan, or Beach SAMP), available on CRMC's website. While one of the main purposes of the CRMC Coastal Guide is to highlight the hazards of coastal living, such as storms, erosion, sea level rise, floods, etc., it does provide an excellent orientation to some of the regulatory issues faced by coastal property owners. And frankly, knowing the hazards of owning coastal properties is an important part of the decision of whether or not to acquire the property. Accordingly, I encourage anyone who currently owns, or is considering purchasing, coastal property to download and read the CRMC Coastal Guide. To some extent, the Coastal Guide covers some of the same ground as this book.

For purposes of much of the discussion in this chapter, I am going to assume that the property at issue is located within two hundred feet of the inland edge of a coastal feature. The importance of that will become clear very shortly, but suffice it to say that this is the trigger for many of the regulations issued by the CRMC.

Regulatory Triggers

There are several regulatory triggers coastal property owners must be aware of and become familiar with. Activities that occur in certain areas trigger CRMC oversight and regulations and generally require a permit, known as an "Assent" if the activities are to be allowed.

The first regulatory trigger to recognize is that the CRMC has jurisdiction over activities within tidal waters of the state, which extend to three nautical miles from shore (a nautical mile is approximately 1.151 statute miles, and a statute mile is of course 5,280 feet). So if you are making an alteration in tidal waters (i.e., waters subject to the ebb and flow of the tide), such as installing a boat ramp, a dock, or a seawall, you will require an Assent.

And be careful here. Tidal waters are not limited to ocean or bay waters. In fact, in Rhode Island, many rivers are tidal for some distance from the coast, and perhaps not even in sight of the coast, and those rivers are subject to CRMC regulatory jurisdiction. Some years back I was representing a client in the construction of a high-rise office building in downtown Providence. It was located in a dense urban area not within sight of the coast. However, in order to construct the building we needed an Assent from the Coastal Resources Management Council. The reason? We were located within two hundred feet of a river barely a few feet in depth. However, it was a tidal river, and it was under the jurisdiction of the CRMC.

The second regulatory trigger is activities occurring a certain distance from the coast. This involves not just a determination of distance, but the identification of what is known as the "coastal feature." If the activity contemplated is within two hundred feet of the inland edge of the coastal feature, it is subject to CRMC regulatory jurisdiction. (As will be discussed below, property can also be subject to CRMC jurisdiction if it is further than two hundred feet from the coastal feature).

By way of example, assume you own a parcel bordering on Narragansett Bay, and you want to construct a gazebo to enjoy sunset or sunrise views over the water, depending on your directional orientation. You carefully measure and locate the structure more than two hundred feet from the high tide line, just to be sure. Are you free and clear? Maybe not. Assume that between your property and the water is a coastal beach, which is a coastal feature. So you measure from the inland edge of the coastal beach two hundred-plus feet for your new gazebo location. Now are you free and clear? Well, perhaps not. Assume the beach runs to a small coastal wetland. That is a coastal feature as well, and you must measure two hundred feet from the inland edge of that feature.

Just to be clear, alternations are not only prohibited within two hundred feet of the inland edge of the coastal feature, they are also prohibited on the coastal feature itself. So if you property includes a coastal beach, that is within CRMC regulatory jurisdiction.

Other coastal features include barrier islands and spits, rocky shorelines, and manmade shorelines, such as seawalls, coastal dunes, and coastal bluffs. Assuming you own property abutting a coastal bluff, and the top of the bluff is 150 feet from the water, CRMC jurisdiction extend 200 feet from the inland edge of the coastal bluff, or 350 from the water.

For more guidance on coastal features, you can go to the CRMC website and print CRMC's guide to Coastal Shoreline Features, which provides significantly more detail on coastal features.

Having determined the coastal feature and the distance, you are only part of the way to determining what you may do and where you may do it.

The third regulatory trigger involves the water type or classification that abuts the property, ranging from Type 1 (conservation areas) to Type 6 (industrial waterfronts and commercial navigation channels). Type 1 waters are the most protected, as one may expect, and what you can do on land bordering Type 1 waters is far more restricted that what you can do on land bordering Type 6 waters.

The other classifications of waters are Type 2, low intensity use, Type 3, high intensity boating, Type 4, multipurpose waters, and Type 5, recreational and commercial harbors. Based on the water types, certain activities pertaining to the waters or adjacent land may be prohibited or restricted or allowed, with there being more regulatory scrutiny the more protected the waters. Bottom line; know the classification of the water abutting your property.

Setbacks and Special Regulations

Once you have determined the limits of the regulatory jurisdiction, you next have to determine whether setbacks apply. These may be construction setbacks and permanent setbacks, and you need to determine whether a buffer zone may be involved. The implication of a buffer zone in particular has significant consequences.

Even if the activity may be permitted within the regulated area, a setback will likely be imposed. For all new structures, the CRMC requires a minimum fifty- foot setback. Section 140 of the Rhode Island Coastal Resources Management Plan (CRMP) provides that a setback is the minimum distance from the inland edge of the coastal feature to the place where the approved activity may occur. The minimum setback shall be the greater of one hundred fifty feet from the inland edge of the coastal feature or twenty-five feet from the inland edge of the coastal buffer zone, whichever is further inland. For example, as discussed above, you would not be able to locate that gazebo closer to the inland edge of the coastal feature than fifty feet, and perhaps further inland if a coastal buffer zone were involved.

Additionally, the CRMC regulates certain areas under special area management plans, or SAMPS, and often calls for increased protection in sensitive areas. Salt ponds have a minimum two hundred foot setback for onsite waste disposal systems and a one hundred fifty foot buffer area for other activities. Lands of critical concern can require increased setbacks of two hundred twenty-five feet for onsite waste disposal systems and two hundred feet for other activities.

Not only are there increased setbacks in special management areas, but there are also elastic setbacks if you are seeking to locate a structure in an area subject to erosion. The setbacks are not fixed measurements, but must be calculated based upon the rate of erosion in the area. If you are building less than four dwelling units, the setbacks are calculated by multiplying thirty times the average annual erosion rate. If constructing more than four residential dwelling units, or if constructing commercial or industrial facilities, the setback is calculated by multiplying sixty times the average annual erosion rate. Thus, if you are building a single-family house in an area where the average annual erosion rate is two feet per year, the setback would be sixty feet (i.e., 2 x 30). If the new structure was a commercial or industrial building or a residential building of four or more units, the setback would be one hundred and twenty feet (i.e. 2 x 60), subject to the minimum required setback as set forth above. Of course, nothing prevents you, except perhaps sufficient land, from increasing the setback to be more protective, but be mindful that you must also comply with local zoning. It is possible you could find that the setback requirement imposed by the CRMC as to the construction of the structure pushed the house closer to the road than allowed by local zoning requirements, requiring you to get a deviation from the municipal requirement. It is also possible to request a variance from the CRMC setback requirements.

The CRMC maintains and uses shoreline change maps to calculate the erosion in the area in order to calculate the setbacks. These are available through the CRMC for review.

Buffer Zones

If the CRMC buffer regulations apply to your property, there is little you can do in the buffer area without getting CRMC permission (RICRMP Section 150 Coastal Buffer Zones). The buffer regulations typically apply to new residential development (for example, the construction of a house on a vacant lot), commercial and industrial development, energy-related activities, and certain public infrastructure. (Section 150 provides that buffer zones for new commercial and industrial structures will be based on their potential impacts on coastal resources.)

The CRMC provides that a buffer zone is an area adjacent to coastal features, which must be vegetated with approved native shoreline species and must be retained in a natural and undisturbed condition. The buffer zone is designed to mitigate the negative impact of human activities on coastal features. It serves as a transition zone between the coast and upland development.

However, as will be discussed below, even if the buffer regulations do not apply to your property, if you are not careful you could make those regulations apply. Obviously, that is something most property owners will want to avoid.

The regulations create a buffer zone on applicable properties, the size of which is based on the size of the property and the type of water the property abuts (one of six categories linked to the condition of the abutting shoreline). For example, a 10,000- to 20,000-square-foot lot on Type 1 or 2 waters requires a fifty-foot buffer zone, while an 80,000-square-foot lot on Type 1 or 2 waters would require one hundred and twenty foot buffer zone. (Variances may be granted from these requirements at the discretion of the CRMC.) That same 10,000- to 20,000-square-foot lot would have a twenty-five foot buffer zone (as opposed to fifty feet) if located adjacent to Type 3, 4, or 5 waters.

Assuming, for example, a seventy-five foot buffer zone from the *most* inland edge of the coastal feature on a property, the property owner would be prevented from altering this buffer in any way, except in compliance with the regulations. The following would generally apply in a buffer zone:

1. Maintenance of vegetation in its natural, undisturbed condition;
2. The planting of native vegetation if the CRMC decided that was required;
3. The filing of a plan for CRMC approval if you wish to prune or trim vegetation; and
4. Restrictions on what you can do in the buffer zone.

The purpose of the buffer zones is to protect water quality, coastal habitat, scenic and aesthetic quality, historic and archaeological resources, and to foster erosion control and flood control.

Given these protections, the regulations for buffer areas are stringent.

For example, pathways that provide access to the shoreline "are normally considered permissible" provided they are less than or equal to six feet wide and follow a winding path that minimizes erosion.

If you are looking to create water views from your new house, "selective tree removal and pruning and thinning of natural vegetation may be allowed within a defined corridor in order to promote a view of the shoreline," but "only the minimal alteration of vegetation necessary to obtain a view shall be acceptable to the Council."

And as to active use of the waterfront area, "minor alterations of buffer zones may be permitted along the shoreline if they are determined to be consistent with the Council's requirements. These alterations may include maintaining a small clearing along the shore for picnic tables, benches, and recreational craft (e.g. dinghies, canoes, day sailboats, etc.) Additionally, the CRMC may allow small, non-habitable structures including storage sheds, boat houses and gazebos...where appropriate."

Note the repeated use of the word "may." The regulations give the CRMC a good deal of discretion to protect the values served by buffer zones.

At this point, if you are feeling pretty good since you own waterfront property that is not subject to the buffer regulations because, for example, your house was constructed before the regulations were applicable to new residential construction, don't get too comfortable. You could actually do something that would result in the buffer regulations being imposed on your property!

More specifically, if you expand the square footage of the foundations of the structures on your property by more than 50 percent, you would be subject to the buffer zone requirements. However, the required buffer will be related to the percentage increase in the foundation footprint, and therefore may not be the full buffer required under the current regulations. The regulations are a bit complicated in this area, so this requires some attention.

When considering expansion of a structure, a property owner should weigh the benefits of the increased structure desired against the restrictions of imposing the buffer regulations on the owner's property and determine what is more important.

Flood Zones and Shoreline Erosion

Flood zones and the importance of flood insurance are discussed in detail in chapter 5. If the property at issue is in a flood zone, it has implications beyond procuring flood insurance, in the event conventional financing was obtained to acquire the property, or if subsequent financing on the property is sought. In particular, there may be more stringent and more expensive requirements for construction imposed under the state building code. If you are in a flood zone A or V, and are building a new structure or substantially improving an existing structure, the building code may well require that the structure be elevated above the base flood elevation, the requirements of which will vary depending on the zone.

Even if the property is not in a flood zone, it may historically have evidenced susceptibility to flooding. The CRMC's Coastal Guide advises that the CRMC maintains Rhode Island Hurricane Inundation Maps, which may have relevance to the property in question.

Related to frequent storms and flooding is erosion at the shore, the dangers of which were demonstrated by the damage and significant erosion to the Rhode Island shoreline caused by Tropical Storm Sandy in 2012. As noted above, the rate of erosion impacts setbacks that restrict the location of new structures, and the CRMC shoreline change maps not only set forth this erosion information, but may provide a guide to property owners of how to be more protective of their property by increasing setbacks beyond applicable requirements to enhance protection of new structures.

Seeking enhanced protection of structures, where feasible, by providing for more-than-mandated setbacks to new construction may be an easier alternative to protecting against shoreline erosion through the addition of shoreline protective features. Such features can include construction of a seawall, bulkheads, or riprap revetments. All such structures are regulated by the CRMC, and depending on the proposed location and adjacent conditions, may be approved or rejected. Reasons for rejection often include potential damage, via increased erosion, to nearby properties, as the made-made protective features protect the property in question but make abutting properties more susceptible to increased erosion. For example, such structures will generally be denied if sought in Type 1 waters or along barriers or if proposed "to regain property lost through historical erosion or storm events" (see generally Section 300.7 of the Coastal Resources Management Plan). Moreover, before granting permission for such erosion control structures, the CRMC will expect that the applicant will "exhaust all reasonable and practical alternatives including, but not limited to, the relocation of the structure and nonstructural shoreline protection methods" (see Section 300.7B). Nonstructural shoreline protection methods include natural vegetation. Given the nature of erosion in some areas of the state, it may be fairly easy to exhaust that alternative.

Other consequences of severe damage is that substantial rebuilding of a structure will trigger current CRMC requirements governing such structures, including setbacks, which could necessitate moving the structure.

Jurisdiction in Regulating Wetlands

Be aware that the DEM and CRMC have reached agreement as to which regulator is authorized to regulate certain wetlands in the vicinity of the coast. As of August 18, 1999, the DEM and CRMC have agreed that the CRMC regulates wetlands in the vicinity of the coast, and the agencies have agreed upon maps, available on their respective websites, which designates wetlands regulated by the CRMC. Table 6A has a list of the cities and towns with wetlands regulated by the CRMC. If the property at issue is located in one of these municipalities, you will want to check the agency maps to see if the wetlands at issue are regulated by the CRMC or DEM.

Municipal Regulations and Potential Conflicts

Currently, both state regulators and numerous municipal regulators exercise jurisdiction over wetlands and onsite wastewater treatment issues, imposing inconsistent and sometimes conflicting requirements. For example, the CRMC regulates all coastal wetlands, and the DEM regulates freshwater wetlands, while the CRMC regulates, by agreement with the DEM, certain freshwater wetlands in the vicinity of the coast. In addition, the DEM regulates onsite wastewater treatment systems, while the CRMC reviews such applications when they are in proximity to coastal features.

At the same time, various municipalities have enacted their own ordinances addressing wetlands and onsite wastewater treatment systems. A recent legislative task force studying the problem of such overlapping regulations found that at least twenty-five municipalities have set their own standards for wetlands setbacks, and the state legislation setting up the task force found that many of these standards are more stringent than the state standards. The purpose of the legislation was to establish a task force to make recommendations, *inter alia*, as to whether wetlands were being adequately protected, whether there were any gaps in the regulatory structure, and recommend standards that would be sufficiently protective so that municipalities would not enact standards that would exceed or contradict the new standards.

That report was issued December 31, 2014, and was addressed by the Rhode Island General Assembly, which passed legislation in June 2015 requiring the establishment of state standards for freshwater wetland buffers and setbacks that prevents municipalities from promulgating their own stricter standards. That legislation amended Rhode Island General Laws 2–1 *et seq.*, entitled Agricultural Functions of Department of Environmental Management, as well as Rhode Island General Laws 45–24 2 *et seq.*, the Zoning Enabling Act.

Upon passage, the legislation effectively prevents municipalities from enacting new regulations to set standards in this area. Once the

Department of Environmental Regulations promulgates regulations setting new standards, the municipalities can't enforce conflicting standards. The legislation also amends the Zoning Enabling Act to prevent municipalities from using their local zoning ordinances to regulate wetlands and buffers.

The legislation does require that the municipalities be informed of wetland permitting proceedings in their jurisdiction, and it allows the municipalities to petition the Department of Environmental Management or the Coastal Resources Management Council (whichever is handling the matter, depending on the location of the wetlands) to seek increased buffer protections. However, this is to be done in a way that does not result in undue delay.

Hopefully, this legislation will go a long way in eliminating the overlapping and often contradictory state and municipal regulation of onsite wastewater treatment systems and wetlands issues that has plagued permitting in Rhode Island for years.

New Construction: Putting Together a Team

Finally, I would note that to the extent new construction or extensive reconstruction is envisioned for a waterfront or coastal property, it is usually necessary to assemble a team of professionals for assistance, preferably those with a track record of working successfully with the regulators in question. This team may include architects, engineers, wetlands biologists, planners, surveyors, environmental scientists, title professionals, etc., depending on the nature of the project and the challenges encountered.

In this regard, it is important to select not only professionals who are familiar with the regulators, but professionals who are well-regarded by the regulators. This last point often goes unnoticed, and I have seen unnecessary delays and overregulation because certain regulators were not entirely comfortable with certain project professionals. Conversely, I have seen projects go much more smoothly when the regulators know they can rely on the science or the judgment or the conclusions of professionals advancing a project.

It is also important to select professionals who will work well together. The last thing an owner needs on a large project demanding teamwork and cooperation is a lone wolf who prefers to go his or her own way and do his or her own thing.

And even though the project may be represented by a knowledgeable and well-regarded lawyer, often it is a good idea to bring in a well-regarded local lawyer who is very familiar with local officials, and local, often unwritten practices or concerns. It is far easier to address a problem when you see it coming rather than when you are blindsided by it.

Table 6A

The coastal municipalities listed below border Narragansett Bay, Mount Hope Bay, and the Atlantic Ocean. The CRMC has jurisdiction over the following coastal towns' certain "freshwater wetlands in the vicinity of the coast" and "coastal wetlands":

1. Barrington
2. Bristol
3. Charlestown
4. Cranston
5. East Greenwich
6. East Providence
7. Jamestown
8. Little Compton
9. Middletown
10. Narragansett
11. Newport
12. New Shoreham
13. North Kingstown
14. Pawtucket
15. Portsmouth
16. Providence
17. South Kingstown
18. Tiverton
19. Warren
20. Warwick
21. Westerly

All other inland municipalities with wetlands are governed only by the Rhode Island Department of Environmental Management.

CHAPTER 7

BOUNDARY ISSUES, RIGHTS TO THE SHORE AND TO A VIEW

his is an important chapter because it is intended to introduce you to some of the problems and pitfalls that may be inherent either in some waterfront properties or in some waterfront property transactions. And that distinction is an important one because it suggests that even waterfront properties that have inherent problems need not end up in purchase and sale transactions that have inherent problems. Problems can be identified and either solved or avoided. Sometimes avoidance of the problem requires avoidance of the property because the problem is not one that can reach resolution on the timeline or on the budget of the purchaser in question. But often problems can be resolved to the satisfaction of the parties, once identified. And that is one of the principal reasons this book has been written, to help buyers and sellers identify problems so they may be resolved. I have seen too much carnage over the years resulting from problems not identified until it is too late. Unfortunately, attorneys are sometimes like ambulance drivers; they get to the scene after the accident.

This chapter focuses on ensuring that the boundary of the property is properly understood, which can be more complicated than it sounds. It identifies the often conflicting rights that arise when waterfront property is at issue, including claimed public access rights, private property easements, and the desire to at least see the water if you have purchased coastal property. Given the complicated nature of laws and regulations pertaining to waterfront properties, some of this discussion is necessarily somewhat technical. I will do my best to avoid or minimize that and when appropriate, simplify it.

Waterfront Property Boundaries

Most prospective purchasers viewing waterfront property they are considering buying assume the property runs to the waterline, and many buy on that assumption. After all, it is waterfront property, and the water must therefore be the boundary. Those who have done no more than make an assumption, or ask the property owner or their realtor, are sometimes surprised to learn that they are mistaken. And the surprise is often an unpleasant one.

This is because waterfront properties can be complicated, there can be different rules for different properties, titles can be peculiar, or physical circumstances could have changed, affecting the boundary. In short, you don't know the property boundary simply by looking at the property.

The Importance of a Survey

Consider the following unfortunate situation briefly mentioned in chapter 4. In that situation, a developer who had owned a waterfront parcel of land in Narragansett since 1984 engaged an engineering firm to prepare a subdivision plan in order to seek town of Narragansett approval to subdivide the property into two buildable lots. That approval was granted. In 2009 the developer sought municipal approvals to construct a house on one of the waterfront parcels. In seeking these approvals, the developer engaged another engineering firm to prepare development plans for the project, which showed property boundaries, the structure, and the individual sewage disposal system.

The developer constructed the house and negotiated a purchase and sale agreement for approximately $1,800,000. The buyer, as a part of his due diligence, engaged a registered land surveyor, Richard Lipsitz, president of Waterman Engineering, to conduct a survey. That survey concluded that the house was wholly constructed on property owned by an abutter, not on the property owned by the developer. Worse, the property abutter was a charitable foundation committed to maintaining its property for public park uses; that binding commitment required the foundation to pay $1,500,000 if it allowed the land to be used for other purposes.

Understandably, the foundation sued for removal of the house, and after several years of litigation, the net result was a lower court order requiring removal and a Rhode Island Supreme Court decision upholding the lower court. The purchase and sale transaction was, of course, cancelled, and the costs of moving the structure are estimated to be between three and four hundred thousand dollars.

The supreme court decision noted that the plan prepared by the engineer for the house construction, which apparently relied on the first engineer's subdivision plan, stated that the "[d]epicted boundary survey conforms with a Class III standard as adopted by the Rhode Island Registration of Professional Land Surveyors." The supreme court further stated in a footnote that according to the Society of Professional Land Surveyors, "a Class III survey is defined as a 'data accumulation survey,' which 'measure[s] and show[s] the relative positions or locations of physical features to a stated graphical scale...'" and that "[t]his definition includes the caveat that '[t]o the extent that property lines are reflected on such plans, they are to be regarded as pictorial only, unless such boundaries are also certified to a Class I, Class II, or Class V standard'" (see *Rose Nulman Park Foundation et al. v. Four Twenty Corp.*, et al., 93 A.3d 25 [RI 2014]).

In other words, do not rely on a Class III survey if you need to know precisely where your boundary lines are located.

And while news reports of this case repeatedly referred to a survey mistake, surveyors are quick to note, quite correctly, that no survey was in fact involved because the plan at issue was prepared by a professional engineer and not a registered professional land surveyor.

As John Mensinger, chair of the Rhode Island Board of Registration for Professional Land Surveyors, wrote in response to a Rhode Island Department of Business Regulation inquiry, no faulty survey was at issue because no survey was at issue. Rather, he stated on behalf of the surveyors Board of Registration that because the survey was not stamped by a surveyor, it was a site plan, but not a survey. The letter goes on to argue that municipal and state regulatory agencies should not accept a site plan where property boundaries must be determined unless it is prepared by a registered professional surveyor.

The lessons for property purchasers exemplified by the *Nulman* case appear clear. First, without the benefit of a survey, you cannot be confident where the property boundaries are located. Secondly, even if something looks like a survey, it may in fact not be a survey. Both courts, in fact, found that even the experienced developer made an innocent mistake in relying on the engineer's site plan. Finally, even if it is a survey, not all surveys will accurately depict boundary lines on which reliance may be placed. A Class III survey will not do so. Accordingly, when purchasing waterfront property, it is entirely prudent to consider, within the facts of your particular circumstance, obtaining a survey stamped by a registered, professional surveyor. In order to accurately locate boundary lines, it should be a Class I, Class II, or Class V survey.

The Precise Boundary Line at the Shore

While a survey will tell you where your property line is, the surveyor must have some instruments of record, such as deeds, or some rules, such as governing case law, telling the surveyor how the line is to be determined.

With regard to property abutting tidal waters, one of the most important determinants of the actual boundary line is a Rhode Island Supreme Court decision, the *Ibbison* case (*State v. Ibbison*, 448 A.2d 278 [RI 1982]).

In *Ibbison*, a waterfront property owner in Westerly sought to prosecute for criminal trespass four fishermen who were engaging in a beach cleanup operation. The property owner asserted that his property boundary extended to the mean high-water line, and that the public could not intrude landward of that line without being guilty of a trespass on private property. Defendants asserted that they had the right to walk up to the high-water mark, being the reach of the average high tide where all the seaweed and drift material is deposited by the tide and accumulates. The state district court found the defendants guilty of criminal trespass, assessing against each of them a fine of ten dollars plus costs. They appealed to the Rhode Island Superior Court, which dismissed the charges, disagreeing with the trial court on the boundary line at the shore. The State then appealed to the Rhode Island Supreme Court.

At issue was an interpretation of Article I, Section 17 of the Rhode Island Constitution, according to the supreme court, noting that Section 17 provides that the people of the state "shall continue to enjoy and freely exercise all the rights of fishery, and the privileges of the shore, to which they have been heretofore entitled under the charter and usages of this state" (*Id.* at 729).

Directly at issue was the determination of the boundary between private property and state land.

As the court posed the question: "To what point does the shore extend on its landward boundary? The setting of this boundary will fix the point at which the land held in trust by the state for the enjoyment of all its people end and private property belonging to littoral owners begins" (*Id.* at 730).

The property owner believed his property extended to the mean high-water line, and the owner staked this line on his property and advised the cleanup crew that they would be trespassing if they crossed this line. The cleanup crew asserted the right to go to the highest high-water mark, which they did and were charged with trespass. The defendants stipulated for the record that they were somewhere between the mean high tide line and the high-water mark and that it was high tide at the time of arrest, so that the mean high tide line was under water.

While this may seem like a lot to do about a little, given that only a couple of feet of beach was at issue, a couple of feet of beach is a couple of feet of beach, and more importantly, if the property owner was right, the cleanup crew would have been prevented from walking on dry sand, since it was high tide and the mean high tide line was therefore submerged.

The court first defined the different boundaries at issue. The mean high tide line was defined to be the average of high water heights over an 18.6 year Metonic cycle. (The Metonic cycle is the cycle of the moon that "begins and ends when a new moon occurs on the same day of the year as it did at the beginning of the last cycle," such that, "at the end of a metonic cycle the phases of the moon recur in the same order and on the same days as in the preceding cycle" [*Id.*at note 2].)

The court stressed that it was deciding a narrow issue, as prior court decisions have made it clear that the shore to which the public has privileges lay between high- and low-water marks. The question therefore presented to the court was how the high-water line is to be calculated. The court relied on common law and prior precedent, including a US Supreme Court decision, *Borax Consolidated Ltd. v. City of Los Angeles*, 296 US 10 (1935), in holding that the mean high tide line was the landward boundary of the shore for purposes of the public's rights to privileges of the shore.

While the court noted that such a boundary unfortunately was not apparent to a casual observer, as the throw of seaweed on the sand would be, it had the benefit of yielding to scientific measurement. The court also found that this approach struck a careful balance between public and private property rights, for if the boundary were the reach of the highest spring tides, it would unfairly take private property from littoral owners that was dry most of the month, and if the boundary were mean low tide it would unfairly constrict the shore available to the public. The court also noted that it was consistent with decisions in a number of other states.

That being said, the criminal trespass charges were dismissed by the court because of question as to whether the trespassers knew the boundary and intentionally trespassed on it (given it was a criminal charge, albeit a minor one, knowledge was important).

The *Ibbison* decision was, in my estimation, a carefully considered decision that was extremely thoughtful in balancing private property rights with the public's rights to enjoy the privileges of the shore. In my judgment, this was another in a series of decisions on waterfront property rights by the Rhode Island Supreme Court over almost two centuries that have gone to great pains to ensure this balance, and in particular, to recognize the importance of private property rights vis-à-vis public access rights.

Based on the *Ibbison* decision, a surveyor can establish the boundary of property fronting on tidal water with precision, and that boundary can be marked and staked.

But that is not the end of the factors that must be considered in determining where the legal boundary line may be established.

Other Boundary Lines

There may be other boundary lines, such as for example where the waterfront property fronts not on the ocean, but on a river, or on a stream, or on a pond. The answer here is that you first start with your deed, just as you do when dealing with property fronting on the ocean. When the deed makes its clear the boundary line is the ocean, a surveyor can stake that line by calculating the mean high tide line. Assume, however, the property fronts on a river. Again, the deed instrument itself will be important. However, if that instrument clearly indicates the property boundary is the river, and if the river is a tidal river (i.e., a river subject to the ebb and flow of the tide), the *Ibbison* rule would apply as public trust lands extend to lands covered by the ebb and flow of the tide, including a riverbed.

Assume that the property fronts on a stream or nontidal river. Again, the deed instruments will be critical in making an interpretation, but the result could be that the property boundary goes to "the thread of the stream" or river, meaning the middle of the stream or river. See *Tyler v. Wilkinson*, 24 F. Cas. 472, 4 Mason C.C. 397 (1827), establishing Rhode Island case law that the owner of land bordering an unnavigable stream owns to the thread of the stream. Surveyors and lawyers will, however, review and interpret the deed carefully. For example, if the deed description says the property runs to the stream or river, it will usually be interpreted as running to the thread of the stream or river (i.e., the middle). If the deed says the boundary is the river bank, or runs to the river bank, or runs along the river, the interpretation may well be that the property does not run to the thread of the stream or river. If the instrument says the boundary runs with the river, it may well be interpreted as running to the thread of the river.

Changes in the Boundary

And what about changes in the boundary line? After all, the shore is dynamic, subject to erosion, storm damage, or even the addition of land by deposits from storms or water conditions. There is case law throughout the country defining what type of physical changes to a shoreline would change the legal boundary between the private property owner and the state. Because there is little case law in Rhode Island addressing this, perhaps surprisingly, given that we are the Ocean State, I will summarize the general rules and then address certain Rhode Island case law.

As a generalization, "natural, gradual and imperceptible changes in the shoreline (such as erosion, accretion and reliction) act to change the boundaries of both the privately owned uplands and the public trust lands" [i.e., state land], while "[n]atural, sudden changes in the shoreline (avulsion), such as those caused by severe storms or earthquakes, do not act to change boundary lines," and "[m]an-induced changes (other than filling) or other modifications of the shoreline by the upland owner, normally do not act to change boundary lines unless a clear legislative grant provides otherwise" (*Putting the Public Trust Doctrine to Work*, Coastal States Organization [2nd edition, June, 1997]).

For clarification, *Black's Law Dictionary* defines accretion as the "act of growing to a thing, usually applied to the gradual and imperceptible accumulation of land by natural causes, as out of the sea or a river." Reliction is defined as an "increase of the land by the permanent withdrawal or retrocession of the sea or a river."

Accordingly, think of slow, gradual, natural changes as resulting in a change in boundary, and natural sudden changes or manmade changes as not changing the boundary line. Filling will be discussed below under Rhode Island law.

As for Rhode Island case law, a Rhode Island Superior Court case provides that land formed by reliction should be divided equitably and noted that authorities have concluded that land formed by means of accretion or reliction should be divided equitably among the riparian property owners (*Shmaruk v. Buser*, C.A. No. 80–1420 [Super. Ct. May 13, 1985]). The court further found that such equitable apportionment should consider two principal objectives, that the parties shall have an equal share in proportion to their lands of the area in question, and an equal share of access to the water and an equal share of the waterline in proportion to their share of the original water line. Here, there is no indication as to whether the land was tidal, and therefore whether public trust issues were involved, but the principle appears to be established that accretion and reliction do in fact change boundary lines.

One may expect that given Rhode Island seems to follow the general rule as to slow, gradual, and natural changes in boundaries, it would also follow the general rule for natural sudden changes, but we will need the courts to tell us that.

The general rules noted above also provided that manmade changes to the shoreline, other than filling, normally do not change the boundary in the absence of a clear legislative grant providing otherwise. The rule in Rhode Island generally follows this, but in a significantly more nuanced way, as is discussed below in the public trust doctrine section.

The Public Trust Doctrine and the Battle for Property Rights

The public trust doctrine has been alluded to in the foregoing discussion of boundary issues, and it requires specific discussion here as it is at the center of disputes between waterfront property owners and the beach-going public.

The Rhode Island State Constitution guarantees shoreline privileges to the public. Article 1, Section 17 reads in full:

Fishery rights—Shore privileges—Preservation of natural resources. —The people shall continue to enjoy and freely exercise all the rights of fishery, and the privileges of the shore, to which they have been heretofore entitled under the charter and usages of this state, including but not limited to fishing from the shore, the gathering of seaweed, leaving the shore to swim in the sea and passage along the shore; and they shall be secure in their rights to the use and enjoyment of the natural resources of the state with due regard for the preservation of their values; and it shall be the duty of the general assembly to provide for the conservation of the air, land, water, plant, animal, mineral and other natural resources of the state, and to adopt all means necessary and proper by law to protect the natural environment of the people of the state by providing adequate resource planning for the control and regulation of the use of the natural resources of the state and for the preservation, regeneration and restoration of the natural environment of the state.

This is known commonly as the public trust doctrine. It is also codified in the Rhode Island General Laws at Section 45–5–1.2. The public trust doctrine is a legal interest held by states in tidal and navigable waters for the benefit of the public. The public trust doctrine is in fact the common law underpinning for our state constitutional and statutory regulation of coastal resources in Rhode Island. In Rhode Island, the public trust doctrine dictates that, "the state holds title to all land below the high-water mark in a proprietary capacity for the benefit of the public...[T]he doctrine preserves the public rights of fishery, commerce, and navigation in these waters" (*Greater Providence Chamber of Commerce v. Rhode Island*, 657 A.2d 1038, 1041 [RI1995]). Therefore, as more specifically discussed above under determining the boundaries of waterfront property, coastal property owners do not necessarily own all the beach and access to the water that extends from their property.

While the public trust doctrine is a doctrine of ancient origin, it is very much a force in Rhode Island today, as the *Greater Providence Chamber of Commerce* decision indicates. The *Greater Providence Chamber of Commerce* case arose from a decision of the Rhode Island Supreme Court, *Hall v. Nascimento*, 594 A. 2d 874 (RI 1991), holding that the creation of new land by filling below mean high tide resulted in the new land being owned by the state as public trust land. In *Hall*, property owners extended their land by placing fill in the sea. The ownership of this property came into question in a mortgage transaction, with dire results for a subsequent property owner, since the septic system serving their property was located on the land that the court found was now owned by the state.

In response to this decision, the then-governor of Rhode Island sought legislation requiring all property "owners" who "owned" land created by placing fill below mean tide to pay a license fee to the state, since the governor claimed the land was actually owned by the state, in reliance on the *Hall* decision. The consequences of this were severe; much of downtown Providence was built on land created by the placing of fill below mean high tide, including college buildings, office buildings, banks, power plants, residences, etc. A number of property owners sued to clear title to this filled tidal land. (By way of disclosure, I represented these property owners and brought the *Greater Providence Chamber of Commerce* case to the Rhode Island Supreme Court.) That lawsuit resulted in the *Greater Providence Chamber of Commerce* decision, in which the court held that land created by the placement of fill below mean high tide, which was done with express or implied governmental approval, or governmental acquiescence, and was so built on and improved as to no longer be suitable for public trust purposes, was owned by the record title owners. The court established a title clearing mechanism to clear title to these parcels. In effect, the court said that the filling of this tidal land under these circumstances extinguished the public trust rights in the land.

In response to this decision, the Rhode Island General Assembly enacted legislation that provides that no title can be acquired in filled tidal lands except by legislative grant unless such title has been acquired "by judicially recognized mechanisms prior to the effective date of this section (July 18, 2000)." It is my understanding, having been consulted during the drafting of that legislation, that the title clearing mechanism set forth by the *Greater Providence Chamber of Commerce* case was such a judicially recognized mechanism as described in the legislation.

That case is emblematic of the interests of many in using the public trust doctrine as a significant public rights weapon. Of course, it sets up a direct clash with private property rights, as we saw in discussion of the *Ibbison* case above. And it is not uncommon for beachgoers to attempt to take over beach area that is in fact located above mean high tide on private property, as many waterfront property owners will attest.

The public trust doctrine, while of ancient origins, as noted, has been the subject of modern efforts to breathe new life and perhaps new meaning into it.

Article I, Section 17 quoted above is not the original constitutional provision. That provision, which was adopted in 1843, originally contained the following language: "But, no new right is intended to be granted, nor any existing right impaired, by this declaration." This language was deleted in 1970 in favor of conservation-oriented provisions, according to constitutional scholar Patrick Conley and former Supreme Court Justice Robert Flanders. This language was reaffirmed at the 1986 Constitutional Convention, which provided that the privileges of the shore included "fishing from the shore, the gathering of seaweed, leaving the shore to swim in the sea and passage along the shore" (see *The Rhode Island State Constitution*, Patrick T. Conley and Robert G. Flanders Jr, 109–120, Oxford University Press [2011]).

To understand the evolution of the claimed public trust rights, it is instructive to look at the Rhode Island Supreme Court decision in *Jackvony v. Powel*, 67 RI 218 (1941). In that decision, at issue was the constitutionality of a public law that allowed the City of Newport to erect fences perpendicular to the shore between Newport and Middletown in order to restrict a popular Newport beach to only Newport residents. The legislation was challenged as being in violation of Article I, Section 17, pertaining to the privileges of the shore.

At that time, the text of Article I, Section 17 was considerably shorter than quoted above. Before its amendment, the constitutional provision then read:

"The people shall continue to enjoy and freely exercise all the rights of fishery, and the privileges of the shore, to which they have heretofore been entitled under the charter and usages of this state. But no new right is intended to be granted, nor any existing right impaired, by this declaration" (*Id.* at 222–3).

The question presented to the court for decision was whether passage along the shore was one of the "privileges of the shore" protected by the constitution. The court could find no case law directly so holding. However, the court noted that *dicta* in some cases (i.e., opinions of the court not binding as legal precedent) seemed to support this, but did acknowledge that some language may have in fact been intended to refer to the right of passage of waterfront property owners *to* the shore, as opposed to *along* the shore. Nevertheless, the court noted that "[a]mong the common-law rights of the public in the shore, which have been frequently claimed by the public or have been described by authors who have discussed the law pertaining to rights in the shore, are rights of fishing from the shore, taking seaweed and drift-stuff there from, going there from into the sea for bathing, and also, as necessary for the enjoyment of any of these rights, and perhaps as a separate and independent right, that of passing along the shore" (*Id.* at 223).

Without being able to find any holdings of the court to that effect, the court concluded, saying, "We are of the opinion that at the time of the adoption of our constitution there was, among the 'privileges of the shore,' to which the people of this state have been theretofore entitled under the 'usages of this state,' a public right of passage along the shore, at least for certain proper purposes and subject, very possibly, to reasonable regulation by acts of the general assembly in the interest of the people of the state" (Id. at 227).

Accordingly, the court held that passage along the shore was a privilege of the shore for certain proper purposes. Given its prior language quoted above, it appears that such proper purpose is to exercise other privileges of the shore, and the court's holding does not go as far as its prior reference that such rite of passage is a separate and independent right claimed by members of the public. And the court clearly acknowledges that such privileges of the shore could be subject to reasonable regulation by the Rhode Island General Assembly.

Fast forward to the 1986 Constitutional Convention leading to the amendment of this Section, where "passage along the shore" is a separate and independent right. That is a case where advocates for beach access rights clearly went further than scholarly judicial opinion would go, and it is indicative of the public pressure to chip away at private waterfront property rights.

The fact is that today there are shore access activists who believe they have a constitutional right to cross private property if that is the only way to walk along the shore. For example, if there is a seawall or elevated bank that does not allow for a natural dry sand area below mean high tide, they believe they have the right to walk along the privately owned seawall or bank. There are others who believe that their right of access includes a right to access to the waterfront across private property. And in fact, some of these access activists have claimed that the public has an easement across the seaward edge of shorefront properties regardless of the location of the mean high tide line. Easements pertaining to waterfront property are discussed below.

Easement Rights at the Shore

Public Easements

Anyone who has dealt extensively with coastal properties is particularly interested in seeing a title search of the property in question, given it is often the case that easement rights may benefit the parcel or may burden the parcel, or both. Often there are easement rights attendant to a right-of-way that many lot owners may use to access the water or a dock.

Often these easement areas are the subject of dispute over the years, as when subsequent purchasers who may be closest to the water believe that easement holders who are using those rights of way are a burden or a nuisance. In fact, such disputes are fairly common and sometimes lead to litigation. There may also be disputes as to the manner of access. Those impacted by the easement (i.e., the servient tenement) may argue that motor vehicle access is no longer allowed, despite the wording of the easement, for environmental reasons or regulatory reasons, or simply because they don't want cars driving through their property.

It is therefore important as part of the due diligence process to carefully review title instruments, and it is important as part of the ownership process to guard your rights, whether as an easement user or an owner burdened by an easement.

The closer one gets to the water, the more heated the easement dispute can become.

Consider a Rhode Island Superior Court decision, decided in September 2014, involving the claim of an extensive easement for the benefit of the public over beachfront property in Westerly (*Kilmartin v. Barbuto* et al., C.A.No. WB-12-0579 [Super. Ct. Sept. 4, 2014]).

In that case, the attorney general brought suit on behalf of the State for the benefit of the public to use a claimed easement over a two-mile stretch of beach in the Misquamicut Beach area of Westerly. Not only was the beach two miles long, but the area in dispute extended between 80 and 120 feet landward of the sea. The claim of public access was based upon the filing in 1909 of a plat that labeled the disputed area as "Beach" and showed public rights of ways leading to the disputed area. The disputed area was not labeled "Public Beach," and the instrument recorded with the plat did not expressly state the area labeled "Beach" was being dedicated for public use, although the designated public rights of way ending at the area designated "Beach" were clearly identified in the written instrument as public.

The motivation for the dispute was obviously the intense interest of the general public in using and enjoying this beach area, which abutting landowners argued was private beach for their use.

The question essentially focused on whether there was sufficient evidence that when the developers of the project filed the plat in 1909, they intended to dedicate the disputed area to the general public for beach use. In an extensive and well-reasoned decision, the trial court, Judge Stern, found that because all of the owners of the disputed area did not sign the plat and instrument recorded in the land evidence records, those who did sign it, no matter what their intention, did not have the legal ability to so dedicate the property. An effective dedication would have required the signatures of *all* of the owners. While this decision was effectively dispositive of the case, the court went on to find there was insufficient evidence of intent to dedicate the disputed area, simply labeled "Beach," and not even "Public Beach," to the use and benefit of the general public.

That case is, however, just one more indication that rights to the shore can get very contentious.

Moreover, it is a warning to waterfront property owners that they must be vigilant in protecting their private property rights at the shore. In Rhode Island, foot traffic over property, no matter for how long exercised, does not ripen into a right of access, whether by a claim of prescription or a claim of adverse use (RI Gen. Laws 34–7–3). However, if this use is not just by foot, but by carriage or motor vehicle, a different result may apply (*Id.*). While easements generally do not arise by virtue of an owner's permissive allowance of someone to use his or her property, absent evidence to the contrary, it could be asserted by the users that the continued use without protest of the owner was evidence of recognition that the user had the right to such use. However, if this were claimed to be a common law license, it could be revoked by the owner, and if not a written easement the claim may well fail. Nevertheless, caution is appropriate.

Also note that in Rhode Island, by statute, there is no right of an easement to air and light. This is important as such an easement could be argued to effectively acquire a view easement, which is often of significant value, certainly at least as to aesthetic value, for coastal property owners who may well want a view of the ocean, coastal pond, or river. By statute, Rhode Island provides that "[w]hoever has erected or may, erect any house or other building near the land of another person, with windows overlooking the land, shall not, by mere continuance of the windows, acquire any easement of light or air so as to prevent the erection of any building thereon" (RI Gen. Laws 34–7–3).

Accordingly, if you are buying coastal property in part for the view, and there is vacant land that if built upon could obstruct that view, or developed land that could be redeveloped within existing zoning ordinances in a manner that would obstruct your view, do not assume you will always have that view nor a legal right to preserve it, beyond relying on existing restrictions of record or compliance with existing zoning and land use ordinances.

Also, as discussed in chapter 9, if there are restrictions on your parcel designed to prevent your property from adversely impacting the views from an abutting or nearby property, or otherwise restricting the use of the property being purchased, be careful, as those restrictions may well be enforceable. If one has acquired coastal property subject to such a restriction, the owner should be diligent in ensuring compliance with the restrictions, as the consequences can be dire, and expensive, for failing to do so, as more specifically discussed in chapter 9.

CHAPTER 8

TAXATION OF REAL ESTATE

D o not judge this chapter by its length. While it is one of the short-est chapters, it is by no means one of the least important. It is important because taxation of coastal properties is a significant element of the ongoing cost of ownership of the property, and it is a cost that is not only increasing, but destined to continue to do so. And it may be a cost that increases faster and higher than comparable costs for other properties in the state. Additionally, it is an area where there are traps for the unwary, such as neglecting to file documents that most property owners do not know exist, let alone know that these documents need to be filed to preserve rights to challenge a tax assessment.

For these reasons alone this chapter merits the careful consideration of anyone considering purchasing coastal property, as well as anyone owning coastal property.

The Problem

When Willie Sutton was reportedly asked why he robbed banks, he is said to have famously replied, "Because that's where the money is." Although Sutton later wrote that he never said the quote, which was supplied by a reporter, he is forever associated with it. And the same rationale explains why coastal property owners are at risk in real estate taxation. The simple fact is that coastal properties are some of the highest valued properties in the state, and tax assessors are well aware of that—just as they presumably are aware of the likelihood that someone who paid a high price for the real estate has the funds to pay high property taxes.

Lest you think this is purely cynical, consider a recent superior court trial, where an expert witness testified under oath for the Town of Bristol in support of his appraisal buttressing the town's position that the property at issue was valued at $1,024,540 (*Newbert v. Spagnolo*, 2006 RI Super. Lexis 90 [July 21, 2006]). The property owner who appealed his assessment owned water-view property. The appraiser for the town used as comparable properties to establish valuation by the comparable sales analysis properties that were waterfront properties, and in doing so, he did not adjust the values downward to be comparable with water-view properties. When questioned under oath, the appraiser testified that he made no adjustment to reflect that certain properties he relied on for comparable were waterfront property, and the subject property was water-view property because some buyers prefer water-view properties to waterfront properties. Incidentally, his appraisal apparently did not note that certain of his subject properties were in fact waterfront properties rather than water-view properties.

In her opinion, the trial justice, Judge Gibney (now the presiding justice of the Rhode Island Superior Court) stated the court had "grave concerns" regarding this comparable sales analysis and found the explanation for using waterfront properties without adjustment to set the value for water-view properties as "disingenuous and unconvincing," noting that "water-front property is consistently found to have a higher worth" than water-view property.

In its holding, the court not only found that the town had overassessed the property by 20 percent, it also found that the methodology used by the town was not supported by a breakdown of statistical evidence used to calculate the assessment, that the expert of the taxpayer was more credible than the expert of the town, and that the town's assessment was excessive.

The lesson here is not the 20 percent differential in taxation, it is that a municipality was using a methodology it did not support statistically to the court, and that the town's expert was advancing a theory that virtually any property owner would reject, namely that there is no difference in value between waterfront property and water-view property. And of course the lack of differential benefited the town, as the town was not trying to assert that lower value water-view property constituted the valuation for waterfront property; it was asserting that higher value waterfront property established the valuation for water-view property.

Word to the wise—be careful with regard to real property taxation.

The Taxation Procedure

In Rhode Island, municipalities assess real estate taxes as of December 31 for the following year (RI Gen. Laws 44–5–1). The assessment is to reflect the full and fair cash value of the real estate, or a specified uniform percentage thereof, such as 90 percent (RI Gen. Laws 44–5–12).

All real property located in the municipality is subject to taxation unless it is exempt. Exemptions will not be discussed here, but if that is an issue, as for example a religious organization owning coastal property for religious purposes, this should be addressed by skilled counsel, as for years the statutory exemptions have been eroded by legislation and court decisions, and the case for exemption must be carefully made and supported.

Most municipalities issue tax bills for the assessment as of December 31 in the following year, often in June or July. Accordingly, real estate taxes are paid in arrears, and at a real estate closing the taxes must be apportioned such that the owner pays the taxes due through the date of the closing, which could result in up to two quarters of taxes being paid at the closing, depending on when it occurs.

Real property is taxed by the municipality in which it is located, and if a property is located in two jurisdictions, it will generally receive a tax bill from each municipality for the portion of the real estate located in that jurisdiction.

Real estate may be valued by three approaches: the market approach, using comparable sales; the cost approach, using replacement or reproduction cost minus depreciation; and the capitalization of income approach, generally used for investment or income-producing property (*Lataille v. Housing Auth.*, 109 RI 75, 280 A.2d 98 [RI 1971]). The Rhode Island Supreme Court has stated that where comparable sales are available, that is the preferred measure of real estate valuation (*Ajootian v. Hazard*, 488 A.2d 413, 416 [RI 1985]).

By statute, a municipality generally may increase the tax assessment from one year to the other by an amount of up to 4 percent over the prior year assessment, although specific statutory provisions allow a higher increase under certain circumstances (RI Gen. Laws 44–5–2). Before one gets too excited by that, keep in mind that annual assessments of 4 percent would double your assessment in eighteen years.

Also note that by statute, municipalities are to do statistical updates every three years and revaluations every nine years (RI Gen. Laws 44–5–11.6). A revaluation is a municipal-wide reassessment of all properties on an individual property basis. Municipalities engage appraisers who visit each property and update the valuation based on changes in the property and changes in the marketplace.

It is extremely important for property owners to understand the difference between a revaluation and an update, as municipalities may cross the line and improperly revalue individual properties during an update.

The State of Rhode Island has promulgated Rules and Regulations for the Implementation of the Triennial Updates and Revaluations to Commence in the Year 2000 through its Department of Revenue.

These "update rules" focus on developing assessment methods to value "each class of property," collecting and maintaining data to develop "value estimates," and analyzing "market influences on the value of land" in order to seek a "goal of uniform assessments." The update rules call for the development of sales ratio analysis and assessment uniformity within a class. The data gathered is to be applied to a class of properties under the update rules.

In other words, an assessor could determine, through supportable market data, that the valuation of all single-family residential properties in a locality had increased by an average of 1.2 percent. That may support a statistical update increasing the assessment of those properties, assuming the data justifies it. But an assessor can't simply decide that a particular waterfront property or water-view property had increased by 10 percent since the last update or assessment. That is effectively revaluing individual properties during a year that is not a revaluation year.

This is not theoretical, as I have seen this happen, and coastal property owners must be vigilant. Often, the justification advanced is that the tax assessor was merely correcting an error. The tax assessor does have the jurisdiction to correct an error in valuation, but that jurisdiction is to correct errors that are clerical in nature. For example, an assessor could correct an assessment recorded of $11,500 when the assessment should have been $115,000, and there was simply a clerical error. But the assessor does not have the jurisdiction under correcting errors or omissions to change the value of the real estate because the assessor's opinion of the value has changed (*Capital Properties v. State of Rhode Island*, 749 A. 2d 1069, 1086 (RI 1999).

Be very careful that in a non-revaluation year, the assessor is not effectively performing a revaluation of your coastal property.

Also, be careful to know your rights during a municipal-wide revaluation. Property owners in a municipality will usually be sent a written notice that such a revaluation is being conducted and that representatives of an appraisal firm will be visiting the property to inspect it. I have also seen notices that implied, or flatly stated, that the property owner must provide the appraiser access to the property and the structure during the inspection. Often the appraiser will leave a card at the door if the property owner is not home, asking the owner to call the appraiser to set up an inspection appointment.

Please be aware that there is no provision of Rhode Island law that requires a property owner to allow the inspector access to its property or structures for such a revaluation. The property owner is free to refuse such access.

Pitfalls for the Unwary

The entire property tax challenge procedure to preserve your rights in the event of an illegal or excessive assessment is fraught with pitfalls for the unwary. They are mostly deadlines—there are a lot of them in the process, and if you miss a deadline, you could be foreclosed from participating in the appeal process or from participating fully in the appeal process. These are discussed below.

There is one pitfall that most taxpayers don't know they have to do every year in order to preserve their appeal rights in certain circumstances.

That is filing a list of ratable estate each year with the tax assessor. A list of ratable estate is your valuation of your taxable property. If a taxpayer files notice of his or her intent on or before January 31 following the assessment of the intention to file an annual account, he or she may file the account between March 1 and March 15 following the date of assessment. Failure to do so prevents the taxpayer from claiming an appeal at the local level, which is a requirement in order to seek court review under the taxing statute, unless the assessment increased from the prior assessment or unless the tax assessed is illegal.

On first glance, this does not appear to be so alarming, as why would a taxpayer appeal if the assessment has not increased. There is one very good reason. Property values may have fallen, so the assessed value may be lower, but the municipality may be seeking more revenue, so it increases its tax rate per thousand to not only recoup the difference in taxes represented by a falling valuation, but to also result in an aggressive tax increase (the taxes paid by the taxpayer are a function of the tax rate applied against the assessed value of the property). Or consider that the assessment may have fallen, but it is still way too high on the market. The taxpayer who did not file a list of ratable estate is without a remedy to contest the valuation amount.

The taxpayer can, however, still contest the tax if it is illegal, but Rhode Island courts have held that a tax that is excessive is not illegal (*Sayles Finishing Plants, Inc. v. Toomey*, 95 RI 471 [1963]). Accordingly, it is prudent for the taxpayer to file a list of ratable estate each year.

Appeal Rights

To challenge his or her tax assessment, a taxpayer must first start at the local level. As indicated earlier, all of these rights are deadline driven, and the taxpayer must be careful not to miss any of the deadlines.

Within ninety days from the day the first tax payment at issue is due, the taxpayer must file an appeal with the local tax assessor. The assessor has forty-five days to make a determination and notify the taxpayer (see generally RI Gen. Law 44–5–26).

In the event the tax assessor fails or refuses to make a determination in the forty-five-day period, the taxpayer can appeal to the municipal tax review board, which must be brought within ninety days of the expiration of the original forty-five-day appeal period.

However, if the tax assessor does render a decision in the forty-five-day period, different rules apply. If the taxpayer is not satisfied with the decision, the taxpayer may appeal to the municipal tax appeal board within thirty days from the date that the assessor makes a determination and notifies the taxpayer.

The board of review must hear the appeal within ninety days of its filing, subject to the right to seek an extension from the director of the Department of Administration. Within thirty days of the hearing a decision must be rendered.

Assuming the taxpayer still is not satisfied, he or she may take an appeal to the superior court within thirty days of notification of the decision by the tax board of review (RI Gen. Laws 44–5–26). If this deadline is missed, the taxpayer can seek to invoke the equity jurisdiction of the superior court if the petition is filed within ninety days of the date the first tax payment is due (RI Gen. Laws 44–5–27).

In the event that the tax assessment is asserted to be illegal or void, the taxpayer can go directly to the superior court seeking remedies provided in R. I. Gen. Laws 44–5–26 and does not have to invoke the local tax appeal procedure (RI Gen Laws 44–5–27).

As I said, there are abundant traps for the unwary in the property tax challenge arena.

Burden of Proof

It is clear that municipal tax assessors have the discretion to determine the value of the property in their jurisdiction subject to taxation (*Willow Street Associates LLP v. Board of Tax Assessment Review, City of Providence*, 798 A.2d 896, 899 [RI 2002]). Tax assessors also benefit from the presumption that they have properly performed their responsibilities until it is proven otherwise (*Harvard Pilgrim Health Care of New England, Inc. v. Gelati*, 865 A. 2d 1028, 1035 [RI 2004]).

Accordingly, the taxpayer has the burden to demonstrate that the tax assessor has valued the property in excess of its full and fair cash value, or uniform percentage thereof as applicable (*Willow Street Associates LLP,*

798 A. 2d at 900). To do so, the taxpayer must present evidence of fair market value, generally through expert testimony, to overcome the presumption that the tax assessor did his job properly and set the appropriate value.

However, as the courts have noted, the tax assessor can greatly help the taxpayer meet his or her burden of proof if the tax assessor presents a flawed methodology without supporting statistical evidence to support the valuation, and the taxpayer can present expert testimony that the tax assessor's calculations and methodology were improper and unsupported (see *Newbert v. Spagnolo*, 2006 RI Super. Lexis 90 [July 21, 2006]).

In essence, the tax appeal cases are often a battle of the experts, and the most persuasive and best prepared appraiser or other real estate professional may carry the case.

The Taylor Swift Tax

If this discussion of property taxation has not been cheerful enough for you, consider legislation introduced by the governor in 2015 as this is being written, dubbed the "Taylor Swift tax," after the popular singer who owns a waterfront mansion in Watch Hill, Rhode Island, which she purchased for seventeen million dollars as a vacation home.

The Taylor Swift tax is an additional tax on real estate valued at over one million dollars and owned by someone living less than six months a year in Rhode Island. The tax rate for this additional tax is $2.50 per $1,000 of valuation. In the case of Ms. Swift, this would cost her an estimated $42,500 more per year in real estate taxes.

It is patterned after legislation originally enacted in 1984 to punish absentee owners of abandoned and derelict properties. That legislation asserted these owners placed more demand on police and fire services, without paying their fair share; left properties derelict without spending money for improvements in order to profit from rising prices; and "must be encouraged to use the properties in a positive manner."

Unbelievably, the Taylor Swift legislation uses the same rationale to tax millionaires who, far from abandoning their property, are lavishing money on it for taxes, insurance, maintenance, security, landscaping, decoration, etc.

If the intellectual underpinnings of the Taylor Swift tax are dubious, what is really going on here? It is nothing more than a naked grab for money without any moral authority. It proposes to collect additional money from certain taxpayers simply because they have the ability to pay it.

And that is the point. As the governor said, the tax "asks those among us who are most able, to pay a little more."

I penned an op-ed for the *Providence Business News* on the Taylor Swift tax, arguing against it and expressing the opinion that the governor was an excellent leader and that in my opinion she would shoot down her own trial balloon and abandon the tax. That is what in fact happened. But the point is, if one is an owner of coastal property in Rhode Island—be careful. While an individual property owner may not be able to prevent passage of ill-advised legislation, the property owner can certainly guard his or her rights to challenge unfair or illegal tax assessments, and should be prepared to do so.

And by the way, this is not an "anti-Rhode Island" sentiment; it simply recognizes that municipal and state governments throughout the country go through boom and bust cycles, and when they are in a bust cycle, they focus on who or what has the resources to help them out—and they are not necessarily looking for volunteers!

PART 3

SELLING COASTAL PROPERTY

This section of the book addresses considerations sellers of coastal property may well want to have in mind as they prepare for a sales transaction. As chapter 9 suggests, sellers should consider whether it is necessary or appropriate to take certain actions in advance of even listing the property for sale, in order to resolve potential issues that could delay or even derail a sale. Coincidentally, just before sitting down to write this introduction, I heard from a client who is a trustee of a trust that owns an undeveloped waterfront lot that the trust intended to market as a single-family house lot for several million dollars. He was contacting me to consider and address issues he thought could impact a sale and should be resolved before marketing the property! Because that trustee was also a veteran attorney, he knew full well the value of properly preparing a significant property for sale. Chapter 9 not only raises these issues for consideration (such as title issues, survey questions, and matters pertaining to the condition of the property and its structures), but it also provides advice on handling the listing agreement and brokerage contract with a realtor. Chapter 9 also addresses how a seller may protect remaining property he or she is not selling when the sales transaction involves only a part of the seller's property. Finally, chapter 10 addresses the sales transaction itself, and in particular the purchase and sales agreement. Provisions important for a seller to consider and present properly are discussed in detail. And because buyer issues often become seller issues, it will be helpful for a seller of coastal property to review chapters 3, 4, and 5, which look at the purchase and sales transaction from the buyer's perspective.

CHAPTER 9

PREPARING FOR THE SALE

S ome preparation by the coastal property owner prior to marketing and selling the property could save time and money, and perhaps avoid lost sales in the process, and could result in a quicker and perhaps more lucrative closing. Surprisingly, it is something to which property owners all too often give too little thought.

The approach is for coastal property owners to understand what prospective purchasers will consider in evaluating their property, and to not only anticipate those issues, but address them as well. Toward this end, this chapter will enumerate a number of issues that a prospective seller may wish to consider before marketing his or her property. Each prospective seller should, however, give this some reflection, as conditions that could impact its sale are often peculiar to the particular property.

Title Search

Anyone purchasing property should do a title search, and buying with lender financing will be required by their lender to do a title search. In essence, the title search shows whether the seller has good and marketable title to the property, and what encumbrances or restrictions may be present. Defects, and some encumbrances and restrictions, could make the title unmarketable, requiring they be cured before conveyance. Other restrictions may not render the title unmarketable, but may impose limitations that make the property undesirable to a particular purchaser. For example, an old, open (i.e., undischarged) mortgage may make the property unmarketable. Problems such as this can often be cleared up, as often it is simply the result of a failure to record a discharge, and the lender will have the obligation to do so when contacted (assuming of course that the mortgage was paid).

Other times, issues may be discovered that cannot be corrected or removed, such as restrictions preventing subdivision. This would not make the property unmarketable, but it may make the property undesirable to a buyer who wants to create a separate lot for a family member to build his or her house. With the knowledge that such a restriction exists, a property owner can avoid marketing the property as one that could be subdivided.

There may also be record title problems, such as old restrictions (for example, access rights to the parcel in question), which could give a buyer pause for concern or even kill a sale. In such cases, with knowledge of the condition, a property owner may be able to get the current title insurer to agree to affirmative coverage for a new purchaser, ensuring that the restriction would not divest the purchaser of title; or, if the enforceability of such restriction was remote, providing affirmative insurance coverage if rights were asserted under the restriction.

If the property has been purchased recently, and the owner has a relatively current, clean title, that may be the end of the inquiry. However, if the property has been owned for years, or has been in the family for generations and passed from family member to family member, a title report prepared by a reputable title company may be a good idea before marketing the property. While conventional wisdom is that property held in a family for generations is the cleanest title, the opposite is often true. I recall a stately family property some years back, located on the water with significant excess land. The son of the owners accepted the recommendation to do a title search before marketing the property, and the search results showed a number of problems that had to be corrected before sale. It took several months to do so, time that in a transaction may have been enough to send the buyer on to another property.

These kinds of title issues are not uncommon, and obtaining a title search is often a prudent precaution before marketing the property.

Survey

Assume the current owner acquired title to the property without a survey having been done. It is not uncommon for purchasers to buy property without a survey, although as discussed above in chapter 4, a survey is often a prudent precaution. It may be a good idea to do a survey, particularly if the property is waterfront, or if it is large and the boundaries have not been clearly marked in the past, or if there are potential encroachments, questions about neighbor boundaries, etc. For example, if the property is burdened with certain access easements or rights of way, showing this on a survey may help purchasers understand the situation, which may relieve concerns. Identifying those issues at the outset, and correcting the ones that can be corrected, may well be prudent.

Assume, for example, that a survey shows that a row of evergreens that the property owner and its neighbor have treated as the boundary line of their respective properties are in fact not the boundary line as shown by the survey. That may well create an issue, because in Rhode Island, under the doctrine of acquiescence, when abutting property owners agree that a physical feature, such as a row of trees, a wall, or a fence is the property line, and that agreement encompasses more than ten years, that could in effect become the boundary as a matter of law. Under those circumstances, assuming a good relationship with his or her neighbor, the property owner may want to correct and document the actual boundary line.

And of course, in the sale transaction, a property owner marketing his or her property can offer the title report and survey to a prospective purchaser, who could get the survey certified and the title report issued to him or her, saving time and money.

Moreover, in the event that a property owner is selling only a portion of the property and retaining a portion, a survey should be done to define the property being conveyed. In any event this likely may be required under the municipal subdivision regulations, if the properties at issue are not already separate legal lots.

Abutter or Neighbor Issues

It is not uncommon for there to be issues involving direct abutters or neighbors that should be addressed before sale. For example, assume a neighbor has been allowed access across the property in question for years, and there is no formal agreement. If the parties want the use to continue, they should formalize it with an easement agreement to be recorded in the land evidence records, spelling out the rights and obligations of the parties. Perhaps the use would detract from the value of the property, in which case they may want to come to some agreement terminating the use.

Speaking personally, I purchased a waterfront property and made it a condition of the purchase and sale transaction that I get an easement from an abutter that was satisfactory to me, given the importance of the easement to the property I was purchasing.

Or perhaps there is an old easement agreement in place, but it raises as many questions as it addresses. In such a case, it may be prudent to negotiate a new easement agreement with the abutter and put that document of record in lieu of the current easement.

Or, as discussed above, if there is an encroachment issue, the parties could agree to its resolution prior to marketing the property and introducing a purchaser to a potential issue.

If a property owner is involved in some running dispute with a neighbor, it makes sense to try to resolve it prior to marketing the property, simply to ensure that it will not be an issue that impacts the sale.

Municipal Issues

To the extent there are any open issues between the property owner and the municipality in which the property is situated, it is a good idea to resolve them. Buyers prefer not to buy problems or disputes. So if there is a pending tax appeal, best to resolve that before going to market. This also applies to disputes regarding zoning, the building code, or other municipal regulations, particularly if they are evidenced by a notice recorded in the land evidence records, as this will show up on any title search. I recall a transaction involving several residential and commercial units on one property that was the subject of an ongoing dispute with the municipality, which required clarity and resolution before the transaction could close.

Property Conditions

You can assume an inspection of the property will be done by a purchaser to include structural, mechanical, electrical, pest, radon, and a well water test if the property is supplied with drinking water from a well. Again, it may be prudent for the property owner to do his or her own inspection, identify deficiencies, and take them off the table. Physical condition of the property is one of the most common sources of termination of the purchase and sale agreement. While it is highly unlikely a prospective purchaser would accept the property owner's inspection and evidence of correction in lieu of doing his or her own inspection, it can level the playing field, as some purchasers use the inspection contingency as a way to renegotiate the price. A property owner would at least have a current report with recent corrections of noted deficiencies, which should negate any exaggerated claims pertaining to the condition of the property raised by a purchaser and should therefore help advance the purchase transaction.

The alternative approach is, of course, to let the purchaser do his or her own inspection and deal with whatever is found at the time. That is a legitimate approach, and perhaps the most common, although it may not be particularly helpful in streamlining the closing process.

With regard to conditions of the property; if a property owner has coastal property with a questionable water supply, this is a problem that is not likely to go away, nor be ignored by a purchaser, and it is one the owner should address head-on. As discussed in chapter 4, it is not uncommon in coastal areas to find homes supplied by well water (or private water systems dependent on well water) for potable water. Such properties can have inadequate supply in summer months, when the population of the community tends to swell, putting the greatest demand on water supplies. In such circumstances, the property owner may want to consider drilling a new or secondary well. This could be used either to supplement the potable water supply or for nondrinking water purposes, such as irrigation, and would lessen demand on the potable water supply.

Flood Plain

As discussed in detail in chapter 5, the location of flood zones in Rhode Island is in flux as a result of FEMA's recent determinations and disagreement with certain of those determinations by the Rhode Island Coastal Resources Management Council. Accordingly, an owner considering selling coastal property may want to check the most recent FEMA maps and any CRMC flood zone maps to be sure that there have not been changes that may result in unpleasant surprises. It is better to know in advance what you are dealing with than to find out in the course of a purchase and sale transaction.

Ownership Entities and Estate Planning

For some owners of coastal properties, the property is the most significant asset they own, and for others, it is just another property. Whatever the case for a particular owner, the sale could have significant tax consequences. Before marketing the property, the owner may well want to consult with his or her lawyer, accountant, and/or estate planner to consider if any changes in the ownership structure should be made prior to sale. For example, it may be important to consider the proposed transfer in the context of estate planning, which may dictate reconfiguration of the ownership entity before sale, or impact the timing of the sale. Whatever the case, trying to fix a problem after it has occurred is more difficult than anticipating the problem and planning for it in advance.

Pricing and Engaging a Realtor

Most sellers rely on a realtor to assist them in setting a market price for their property, and often this works quite well. There can, however, be considerations with this approach that suggest alternatives.

For example, some years back I knew a realtor who specialized in a particular area of a particular city, and I noted how quickly her listings sold—often within days of the initial listing. The houses were in an older, established neighborhood where families had lived for years, and had recently become very popular. It occurred to me that the houses were being sold below market by this realtor. Often, the listing realtor also brought the buyer to the transaction. The sales went quickly, which commonly happens with below-market sales. Assuming this was the case, the sellers, who had been in their homes for years, would make a nice profit, but not necessarily the profit the market would suggest was due. And the realtor would be quite happy, because this realtor was often on both sides of the transaction, and the commission was a small part of the sale price, and therefore, any "lost" commission on the differential between market price and sale price would be very small. The quick sale, and the ability to bring a buyer to the transaction, would more than make up for the loss in commission.

On the other side of the issue, it is not unheard of for a realtor to give a high prospective marketing and sale price in order to get the listing, and then let the market educate the buyer, with resulting price markdowns until the property sells. If an owner is considering two realtors, and one says the property should sell for $2,000,000 and the other says the property should sell for $2,500,000, human nature may drive the seller to the realtor suggesting the higher price.

To avoid this bias, another approach would be to hire an appraiser to give a formal appraisal of the property. Appraisers are trained in valuation, they have standards to follow, and they are not seeking the listing (note, however, that some good appraisers also have realty companies). For a few hundred dollars you will have a report with comparable sales comparisons and a recommended market price. This certainly would provide more information for your discussions and negotiations with realtors. Be advised, however, that it is not uncommon for an appraiser valuing a unique or special coastal property to consult with a good realtor to get his or her take on market price, since the value of what someone will pay for a special property is often decided not by the market, but by the buyer. One excellent appraiser told me that he once appraised a spectacular coastal property, and it subsequently sold for substantially more than the appraised value, and more than realtors thought it would. Beauty is, in fact, often in the eyes of the beholder. Caution, therefore, is advised. The more special the property, the more difficult it is to value.

Regarding contracting with a realtor, the property owner and the realtor have directly conflicting interests. The property owner would like to pay as small a commission as possible; pay a commission to only the realtor who sells the property; have the flexibility to use as many realtors as possible; obligate the realtor to spend generously on advertising; and contract for as short a listing period as possible, preferably with the opportunity to terminate at any time. The realtor, on the other hand, wants a contract for as long as possible, with no ability of the seller to terminate early; wants to receive a commission no matter who sells the property (including if the property owner sells it on his or her own to a relative); receive as large a commission as possible; and incur the least possible costs.

That, of course, means that each should be looking for something different in a contract than the other is offering or suggesting. For example, I was recently assisting someone seeking to buy a property. A realtor, in the same office as the realtor listing the property, wanted a six month exclusive contract to represent the buyer for this purchase or any other purchase during that six-month period. That exclusive meant that if the buyer bought any other property in the state, which sale arose during the six month contract, the realtor would get a commission—even if the realtor was not involved in the sale in question. I advised the buyer to agree only to an exclusive for the property in question for a three-month period. The agent refused to represent the buyer under those circumstances. I then advised the buyer to direct the realtor to simply convey the buyer's offer to the listing agent, and the realtor was then out of the situation (i.e., no commission). And of course, under those circumstances, the agent saw the wisdom of signing the limited agreement.

Accordingly, property owners should not just sign the standard form agreement a realtor presents. Everything about the transaction is subject to negotiation, and there is therefore no standard form contract. Negotiations should include: whether it will be an exclusive contract or a nonexclusive contract; what advertising and marketing the realtor will do; what expenses he or she will incur; what commission the realtor will earn; the duration of the contact, etc. These and other matters should be subjects of discussion when comparing brokerage firms. What is their marketing plan? Will they advertise in the *Wall Street Journal, New York Times*, and other outlets? Will they do a professional video? A brochure? What is the notice period prior to a showing, and what is the realtor's showing procedure? If the coastal property is a vacation home the sellers uses only on summer weekends, a realtor who plans on open houses and showings on the weekends should meet resistance from the owner. What is the ability to terminate the realtor's services? What budget is he or she proposing, and how are the expenses allocated? What is the marketing plan? Who are the realtor's target buyers, and how is he or she going to reach them? How do does the realtor qualify buyers? A seller wants to know that his or her realtor is active, not passive, and has a real plan for the property. Answering the phone when it rings is not a marketing plan! And, the seller wants to know that the realtor is on the same wavelength with regard to the selling price, marketing plan, showing procedures, etc.

There are some excellent realtors working high-end properties, and a seller wants to be sure that he or she has one under contract, and that the contract is one that gives the realtor the flexibility and incentive to perform while also giving the seller the control needed to ensure the transaction proceeds in his or her best interests.

With regard to the listing, one of the services a good realtor performs is to ensure that the listing agreement is thorough and accurate and that it fairly describes the property being marketed. This necessarily includes an accurate and thorough description of what is being conveyed, and very importantly, an accurate and thorough description of what is not being conveyed. The seller should discuss this in detail with the realtor and ensure that specialty furnishings, such as chandeliers and candelabras, which might normally be considered fixtures that convey, be excluded if they do not convey. Items such as draperies, window treatments, etc. that may or may not convey should also be specified. I was involved in the sale of a high-end coastal property where the listing broker had failed to do this properly. It caused negotiation issues between the buyer and the seller, and the listing agent's commission was ultimately adversely impacted. While these matters can be corrected at the purchase and sale agreement stage, it can have an adverse impact on the seller's pricing and should be gotten right at the outset.

Protecting Remaining Property

While it is not the usual sale, it is not uncommon for a seller to sell part of his or her property and retain the remainder for continued use. For example, a property owner may have a six-acre property improved with a single-family residence in a zoning district where the minimum lot size is two acres. The seller may decide to sell a two-acre parcel for development of a single-family house. In doing so, the property owner could impose restrictions on the parcel being sold to protect and benefit the property being retained.

For example, if a coastal property owner is selling one of two lots, he or she can impose restrictive covenants on the lot being sold to protect the view of the remaining property. This can be important for maintaining or enhancing the value of the property being retained. It can also be important for purchasers of such a restricted lot to ensure they abide by the restrictions. A recent Rhode Island Supreme Court decision demonstrates both these principles.

In *Cullen v. Tarini*, 15 A. 3d 968 (RI 2011), the Rhode Island Supreme Court upheld a plaintiff's efforts to enforce a restrictive covenant the plaintiff placed on a property before selling it in order to limit the location, size, and height of any structure that could be built on the land being sold.

The reason? In the words of the court, the property the plaintiff retained and did not sell "is very nearly the highest point on Aquidneck Island" with "a grand vista that looks out to the south and the southeast that has direct ocean views that are spectacular." Construction on the property that the plaintiff was selling had to be limited in order to prevent it from blocking the ocean views of the property the plaintiff was retaining.

When the first purchaser found that plaintiff would not modify the restrictions, they sold the lot without constructing a residence. The new buyer was less reserved.

The new buyer engaged a designer/builder to construct a significant residence, but according to trial testimony, did not advise the designer of the restrictive covenants of record limiting construction (such as size and height), and only advised him that the house should be built in a designated area, but that these were "general guidelines only."

The buyer did have discussions with the plaintiff and even showed him plans for the new residence, but the plaintiff said that the plans were insufficient for him to understand that they violated the restrictions, and the buyer did not tell the plaintiff that his plans violated the restrictions.

The ensuing construction under the plans would have exceeded the height limitation, square foot limitation, and location limitation of the restrictive covenant. When the plaintiff became aware of the violations, the plaintiff sued for an injunction, which was granted. At that point, the new buyer had spent $1,250,000 on construction of the partially completed residence.

The trial court found for the plaintiff and ordered the offending construction removed, in such a manner that it no longer violated the restrictions. The supreme court upheld that decision, rejecting a number of challenges.

Significantly, the court found that in order to enforce restrictive covenants, it was not necessary to make a separate finding of irreparable harm to the plaintiff. Quoting from the Restatement (Third) of Property Law, the court said, "[T]he value of a restrictive covenant often is subjective and difficult to evaluate in monetary terms. For this reason, injunctive relief is an appropriate remedy so long as the purpose for which the restrictive covenant was created continues to exist."

The court also found that it was not necessary to balance the equities between plaintiff and defendant in a restrictive covenant case, as "proof of a violation of a restrictive covenant was sufficient for a court to grant injunctive relief."

An existing coastal property owner considering selling a portion of his or her coastal property for development should certainly consider the use of restrictive covenants, when appropriate, to protect water-view property or other important view corridors and property interests. If one has acquired coastal property subject to such a restriction, the owner should be diligent in ensuring compliance with the restrictions, as the consequences can be dire, and expensive, for failing to do so.

CHAPTER 10

THE SALES TRANSACTION

I n order to get the most out of this chapter from the seller's perspective, please go back and review or reread chapter 3, discussing the negotiation, offer, and purchase and sale process primarily from the perspective of the purchaser. That discussion will not be repeated or even summarized here, but it provides background for the discussions in this chapter (which will be truncated given the discussions in chapter 3). In this chapter I primarily focus on considerations unique to the seller in the sales transaction.

Engage Legal Counsel

At the risk of the suggestion that I am promoting lawyers, I reiterate the recommendation regarding engaging legal counsel for the transaction, and that this ought to be done early in the process. In the case of the seller, that engagement may want to come before a purchaser enters the picture and begins negotiating a transaction. This is particularly true if the seller follows the advice given in chapter 9 to prepare the property for sale, as is hoped, and in the course of doing so, discovers issues such as title problems or municipal issues that should be addressed before the property is actually put on the market.

To the extent there is concern pertaining to conditions of the property that could be serious, such as environmental issues, it may be helpful to have counsel undertake investigation and engage experts and other professionals as necessary. This may also have the benefit of bringing any material produced in the investigative process under certain protections from court discovery, such as the attorney work-product protection. For example, experts engaged at the recommendation of a lawyer to assess certain matters in anticipation of litigation, and who produce material pertaining to this engagement, may be protected from disclosing this material to the other side in the event there is litigation relative to the condition and the material is subpoenaed. Had the seller simply contracted for the study, all of the information produced may be discoverable in the litigation and could adversely impact the seller with regard to liability. Of course, it is hoped that the process will not result in litigation, but when that appears to be a possibility, it is best to take precautions.

The Offer

In chapter 3 I discussed the pros and cons of a purchaser doing a separate offer followed by a purchase and sale agreement, or simply moving right to a purchase and sale agreement and skipping the offer. While there is no right or wrong here, I expressed a preference for skipping the offer, and I would take the same position with regard to advising the seller as well. However, if the market is active, and the transaction is time-sensitive, a seller may legitimately express a preference for taking offers and deciding among them to ensure he or she is selecting the most motivated purchaser who is most likely to consummate the transaction. However, that may not be the usual circumstance, and normally, moving to a purchase and sale agreement can make sense.

The Purchase and Sale Agreement

There are several terms of the purchase and sale agreement to which a seller should be particularly sensitive, which I will note briefly here. Of course, all of the business terms are important, and by highlighting several I am not suggesting that the others be ignored. Rather, these are terms that particularly impact sellers and should be subject to careful consideration.

Purchase Price and Its Payment

While the sales price is, of course, important, sellers normally don't need a lawyer to tell them to pay attention to the purchase price. But what may require some consideration is the circumstance where a purchaser requests seller financing, meaning that the seller takes a portion of the purchase price by payment of a promissory note, payable on certain terms, often secured by a first or second mortgage on the property being sold. There may be a number of reasons for this request, ranging from the temporary illiquidity of the purchaser to the inability to properly finance the property in the current real estate financing market. The seller should, of course, understand the reason for the request, assuming, of course, it was not a seller initiative to facilitate sale of the property or to facilitate a sale at an above-market price.

Beyond the reasons for the request, which may reveal additional risk factors, a seller should consider whether he or she in fact wants to be a lender, because that is what granting seller financing means. As a lender, you get a return (i.e., an interest rate) in exchange for accepting risk, receiving payment that is either not timely, or not full, or both. A seller must decide what the risk level is and how the return compares with that risk. The primary risk, of course, is not being paid as and when promised and having to chase the borrower, or exercise remedies under the promissory note and mortgage. These remedies could range from foreclosure to foreclosure and suing for a deficiency. And if the seller is a second mortgagee, meaning seller's mortgage is junior to the purchaser's bank financing, the seller would have to pay off the purchaser's financing to acquire the property. Further, if the senior lender foreclosed, the seller's mortgage, and thus its security, could be wiped out.

Equally as important, a seller must decide whether he or she wants to spend the time and energy to be a diligent lender (being a non-diligent lender is a little like being a careless skydiver; you are squaring the risk of something already risky). This involves not just documenting and confirming the creditworthiness of the borrower, and perhaps as importantly, his or her character, but it also involves paying attention to ensure the collateral (i.e., the property that is sold) is protected. The seller, as a mortgagee, must require property and casualty insurance, on which the seller is a lost payee, and should also require comprehensive general liability insurance.

The seller, as a mortgagee, must ensure the insurance is sufficient, it is being maintained, the seller is getting notices of renewal, and the seller will receive advance notice of cancellation. The seller, as mortgagee, must also ensure there is no "waste" of the property, and that it is being properly maintained. The seller, as mortgagee, should also consider restrictions in the mortgage on what may not be done on the property (including alteration of the structure, new construction, etc.), and must ensure these restrictions are being observed. All of this takes a certain amount of time and attention.

So while it may seem like a good idea to have a stream of income for a number of years after the sale (i.e., repayment of principal and interest under the promissory note), being a lender is not for the faint of heart and not recommended unless the seller is a savvy businessperson with some appetite for risk.

Due Diligence

From the seller's perspective, there are several concerns if the purchaser is conducting any material due diligence, such as that pertaining to environmental issues. A seller wants to ensure that everyone who accesses his or her property has insurance (comprehensive general liability and property damage) and that no activity can be engaged in without the seller's approval. If there is going to be any significant testing, such as for environmental considerations, including test borings, the seller will likely want to have a separate access and indemnity agreement. While such testing is not normal in residential transactions, it can arise given the nature of the property and its conditions, and it should be expressly addressed in a specific agreement and not left to provisions in a form agreement. For example, you want to control the type of testing. One can do test pits with an auger or with a backhoe. Obviously, if it is your property, you want the auger and not the backhoe. Again, these issues generally arise in the context of commercial real estate transactions, not residential, but they are not unheard of in residential transactions, particularly when significant acreage may be involved.

A seller should also be concerned about the time period for due diligence activities. The Rhode Island realtor's form agreement provides for ten days. That may be adequate in most circumstances, but it may not be adequate if the property is extensive or if there are issues peculiar to the property. That being said, a seller benefits from as short a period as is reasonable, as it is a contingency that could derail the transaction, and if that is going to happen, a seller wants to know it sooner rather than later. I have seen some sellers give an extended period for due diligence, only to regret it later.

Status of Title

In the event that a seller has not taken the advice in chapter 9 to have a title search done of his or her own title to the property as part of the preparation to sell the property, it is strongly recommended that the seller not agree in a purchase and sale agreement to correct any defects of title. The reason is that a purchaser's title search may reveal defects that are extremely expensive and/or time-consuming to cure, and a seller should not commit to that in advance without knowing what may be at issue. The provision should simply give purchaser the right to terminate if seller does not cure the defect. Also, a seller should be aware that the standard form purchase and sale agreement used in Rhode Island essentially allows a purchaser to raise title issues on the day of the closing. I strongly recommend that if this document is used, it be amended to require that the purchaser conduct the title investigation with ten to perhaps fifteen days after signing the agreement, in order to raise title issues early on in the process. Waiting until the end of the process can result in the purchaser using a minor title issue to terminate the transaction, or exerting leverage to require a prompt, but more expensive, correction of a title defect.

Contingent on Purchaser's Sale

A purchaser will often make his or her obligation to purchase contingent on the sale of its current residence. This is often accepted by sellers. Some caution is warranted here. If a seller is willing to accept this contingency, there should be an absolute drop dead date when the seller has the absolute and unconditional right to terminate the transaction if the transaction has not closed. Absent that, the seller is being held hostage to a transaction that is outside his or her control and could take months to close, or may not close at all. The wording in the contract regarding the seller's right to terminate should be unequivocal.

Pre-Closing Occupancy

Occasionally in a residential real estate transaction a purchaser will propose renting the property prior to the closing. There can be any number of reasons for this, ranging from a delay in the anticipated sale of purchaser's property, which it needs to close in order to close the purchase transaction, to the need to complete permitting to substantially remodel the property being purchased. From a purchaser's perspective, many of these may be good ones. From a seller's perspective, almost none are.

In essence, in granting such a request, the seller has effectively taken its property off the market without a sale and also has someone occupying his house. If the purchaser defaults under the purchase and sale agreement, the seller may be now dealing with a hostile tenant, possibly an eviction action, and perhaps waste or damage to the property. A seller should think long and hard before agreeing to a pre-closing lease. (And many times the realtors will be pushing it, for fear that the deal, and their commission, will disappear without it.)

Remedies on Default

The realtor's standard form purchase and sale agreement essentially provides each party with all available legal and equitable remedies in the event of default. One of these purchaser remedies is specific performance. Specific performance is the right of a purchaser to sue a defaulting seller to force the seller to sell the property to the purchaser. This, of course, sounds fair and reasonable. After all, the purchaser (or his or her realtor or attorney) argues, the purchaser has spent time and money in due diligence and inspections to acquire the property, the purchaser has done everything he or she was required to do under the purchase and sale agreement, and the seller should not be able to breach the contract, refuse to sell the property to the purchaser, and simply return the deposit. The purchaser will further argue that without such a right of specific performance, after signing the contract with the purchaser, and causing the purchaser to spend money in reliance on the purchase and sale agreement, the seller could accept a last-minute offer for a higher purchase price and walk away from its contract, with his or her only obligation being to return the deposit.

While that certainly sounds like it would be unfair and unreasonable, consider another scenario. The purchaser and seller get into a dispute after signing the contract, arguing over certain contingencies or the meaning of certain terms. Assume further the purchaser refuses to close unless seller undertakes certain action that purchaser claims is required, perhaps remediating what may be insulation containing asbestos, and seller asserts the insulation does not contain asbestos and this expensive remediation is not required under the contract, and terminates the agreement for purchaser's default in refusing to close. Even if purchaser has an unsupported position under the purchase and sale agreement, the purchaser could still sue the seller for specific performance, and file a *lis pendens* in the land evidence records against seller's property. A *lis pendens* is notice to third parties that the purchaser is suing to enforce an equitable interest in the property, which will effectively prevent seller from selling the property. It could take years to resolve the litigation, and the purchaser could use that to try to force concessions from seller or the payment of money from seller.

This is not uncommon.

Accordingly, a seller may wish to revise the standard form purchase and sale agreement before signing to provide that the purchaser has no right of specific performance, and in the event of default, the purchaser's remedy is return of the deposit. Alternatively, the seller could agree that if the seller willfully refuses to close and terminates the agreement, and this is not excused by the purchaser's breach, the purchaser is entitled not only to a return of its deposit, but to repayment of all out-of-pocket expenditures the purchaser made in furtherance of the transaction, and that if the purchaser is required to sue to enforce his or her rights, he or she also will be reimbursed for attorney's fees. This is a much better provision for a seller than a purchaser's specific performance remedy, and it is also fair to the purchaser.

Options and Rights of First Refusal

While options and rights of first refusal are not usual in the residential real estate transaction, they sometimes arise in significant coastal property transactions where all of the real estate is not being sold. I recall in one significant coastal property transaction, the purchaser's insistence on having a right of first refusal on the seller's abutting property effectively killed the transaction, as this particular seller did not want the entanglement. That seller's instincts were good, and most sellers should be very wary of granting such rights.

An option to purchase is usually a negotiated right to buy certain property at a specified price and on specified terms. I have seen bare-bones options, where there is little mentioned other than the price, but they are an invitation to a dispute, if not litigation, and are to be avoided. A purchaser will often argue that he or she wants the ability to buy the property a seller is retaining and that abuts the property being purchased. In the typical situation, the holder of the option is in the driver's seat, and he or she may decide to exercise the option and purchase the property, or waive the option and not do the deal. The seller/owner is the party burdened, and this is one of the reasons that I suggest sellers not enter option agreements for property being retained.

In the event the seller decides to do so, it is important to make the option as detailed and specific as possible, so there is little left to dispute. For example, I suggest that the option agreement also contain all the terms of the purchase and sale transaction, so if the option is exercised there is no need to negotiate a separate purchase and sale agreement, which can lead to disputes. In the event of a dispute, the option holder can bring suit, put a *lis pendens* on the property (i.e., a record notice of litigation involving title to the property), which will prevent the seller from selling the property until the dispute is resolved.

Alternatively, a purchaser may request a right of first refusal rather than an option. A right of first refusal is an agreement where the seller commits to give the holder of the right an opportunity to buy the property on the same terms the seller is willing to sell to a third party. The holder is generally given the opportunity to elect to purchase for a limited period of time, and if the holder does not elect to purchase, the right generally terminates unless the property is not sold within a specified period of time. If that time is exceeded, the seller has to once again offer the property to the holder on the then-current terms and conditions being offered to third parties.

I generally advise sellers to avoid giving rights of first refusal as well, for several reasons. First, given the nature of rights of first refusal, they make it difficult for a seller to easily determine if the holder of the right will actually purchase the property. For example, a seller could decide on what terms he or she wishes to sell the property, present the terms to the holder of the right, and be told that he or she is not interested in purchasing the property. After months of unsuccessfully trying to sell the property, the seller may discover that the terms are above market terms. When the seller revises the terms to meet market conditions, he or she will then have to re-offer the property to the holder of the right. That can be cumbersome and time-consuming, and it effectively pushes the seller to wait until he or she has a valid offer before presenting it to the holder of the right of first refusal. This is disadvantageous as it forces the seller to negotiate the deal with one party, then take it to the holder of the right of first refusal to see if he or she is interested, and it may discourage the prospective purchaser from even dealing with the seller, knowing that he or she could be negotiating a transaction that turns out to benefit the holder of the right of first refusal instead of him- or herself.

These transactions can also lead to litigation, as where the seller presents the offer to the holder of the right, the holder rejects it and decides not to buy, and the seller and a purchaser later negotiate slightly different terms. The holder of the right then sues because he or she claims that were he or she presented with the slightly different terms, he or she would have elected to purchase.

If a seller is leaning toward granting one of these rights because a purchaser is insistent, I sometimes suggest a third option: a right of first offer. Under this approach, the only obligation of the seller is to approach the holder of the right to inform the holder that the seller intends to market the property. The seller asks if the holder is interested in purchasing, and if so, on what terms and conditions. If the two parties are unable to come to an agreement within a specified period, such as ten days, the right terminates, and the seller is free to market the property to third parties. This obviously does not give the holder all the benefits of an option or a right of first refusal, but it does give the holder the opportunity to negotiate a deal. From a seller's perspective, it avoids the potential liabilities inherent in an option or in a right of first refusal.

Disclosure

In chapter 4 there was a discussion of the real estate sales disclosure act, primarily from a purchaser's perspective, although it is obviously the seller that is required to make the disclosure. Here I want to focus on the disclosure from the perspective of the seller. The Rhode Island Supreme Court has considered in two decisions in the same case the obligations of the seller to make disclosure under the Rhode Island Real Estate Sales Disclosures Act (RI Gen. Laws 5–20.8–1 *et seq.*). In that case, a purchaser brought suit against a seller, the seller's real estate agent, and the purchaser's real estate agent for failure to disclose that the waterfront property at issue was subject to severe erosion (*Stebbins v. Wells*, 766 A. 2d 369 [RI 2001] [*Stebbins I*] and *Stebbins v. Wells*, 818 A. 2d 711 [2003] [*Stebbins II*]).

While those decisions are particularly important for real estate agents (as the court found that agents have a duty under the Disclosure Act, independent of their client, to disclose matters required to be disclosed by the Disclosure Act), the decisions are important for sellers as well.

The court found that while caveat emptor is essentially the guiding principle under Rhode Island law as it pertains to real estate purchase and sale transactions (meaning that the buyer is responsible for informing him- or herself as to the quality and condition of the property being purchased), "passive concealment by the seller" is an exception to the rule of caveat emptor. In *Stebbins I*, the court remanded the case for trial on the question of whether the erosion condition on the property was ordinary erosion of waterfront property, which would not be required to be disclosed as it would not be a defect but usual and normal, or whether it was "far more severe than ordinary erosion," which would rise to a defect that would be a required disclosure.

Sellers take note: if it is out of the ordinary, it is a required disclosure.

The court in *Stebbins II* also addressed the issue as to whether there was an implied cause of action in the Real Estate Disclosure Act allowing a lawsuit for damages in the event of breach, or whether the remedy in the act for breach, a penalty of one hundred dollars, was the sole statutory remedy. The court found that there was no implied cause of action for damages under the Disclosure Act, and the statutory remedy of a one hundred dollar penalty was the only remedy under the statute.

However, sellers should not celebrate and assume they can breach the Disclosure Act with impunity, given that the penalty is so low. The *Stebbins II* court also found that a breach of the Disclosure Act could be "cited as breaches of the seller's legal duty to disclosure" in support of any negligence claims against the seller. In other words, a disappointed purchaser could sue a seller for negligence, and seek damages for such negligence, citing as proof of the negligence the seller's breach of the Disclosure Act. And of course, damages for negligence would not be limited to one hundred dollars as in the Disclosure Act, but could run into tens of thousands of dollars or hundreds of thousands of dollars, depending on the proof of actual damages offered.

The bottom line for sellers is to pay careful attention to the disclosures required to be made by the Disclosure Act, and when in doubt, err on the side of disclosure.

Form of Deed

Most sellers give absolutely no thought to the form of deed by which they will convey their property. The standard form of deed in residential real estate transactions is the warranty deed. The significance of the warranty deed is that the seller warrants the status of title to the purchaser. By statute, these warranties include that the seller "is lawfully seised in fee simple of the granted premises," that the property "is free from all incumbrances," and that "the grantee and his or her heirs and assigns shall at all times hereafter peaceably and quietly have and enjoy the granted premises" and that the seller "will warrant and defend the premises to the grantee, and his or her heirs and assigns forever" (RI Gen. Laws 34–11–16).

This includes not only title matters arising during the seller's period of ownership of the property, but matters arising in the chain of title years before the seller's ownership of the property. And it is not a theoretical warranty. A purchaser can actually sue his or her seller years later for an alleged breach of one of the warranties of title. Note the last quoted warranty above about defending the title.

To the extent that there are incumbrances or defects in title that the purchaser has accepted, these can be excluded from the warranties by noting them in the deed as exceptions. Therefore, there are very good reasons for sellers to be careful about the status of title to the property being sold, particularly if the seller is giving a warranty deed.

Also, note that if a purchaser had an issue with the status of title, while the purchaser could sue the seller under the warranties given in the seller's deed, the purchaser would likely also sue the title insurer, or at least make claim against its title insurer, and the title insurer may resolve the claim. In this regard it is important to understand that there are matters that title insurance specifically does not cover, and if the defect in title is one of those exceptions from title insurance, the purchaser has every incentive to sue the seller under the deed warranties.

An alternative for a seller is to give a statutory quitclaim deed instead of a warranty deed. By statute in Rhode Island, a statutory quitclaim deed is effectively what is known as a special warranty deed in other jurisdictions. It provides warranties of title, but only pertaining to matters that arose during the period of ownership of the seller. In other words, if the seller owned the property for ten years, and there was a defect in title that arose twenty years ago, the seller's quitclaim warranties would not cover that. This reduces the exposure of the seller and arguably confines the seller's liability to something the seller should know about—matters arising during the seller's ownership. Statutory quitclaim deeds are commonly accepted in residential transactions and are the usual deed tendered in a Rhode Island commercial transaction.

Rhode Island also recognizes a bargain and sale deed, which does not contain warranties of title, but are not common in residential real estate transactions in Rhode Island and would likely meet confusion at best, and resistance at worst, in a residential transaction.

And hopefully, if all the advice in this book is taken, once the deed is delivered and the consideration is tendered, seller and purchaser will live happily ever after!

ABOUT THE AUTHOR

J ohn M. Boehnert practices real estate, real estate development, and environmental law in Providence, Rhode Island, including coastal permitting, waterfront property rights, and public trust doctrine issues.*

His clients have included developers, energy companies, multinational corporations, investors, lenders, nonprofit corporations, individual property owners, and state and local governmental entities. He has represented one of the world's largest energy companies on environmental and real estate issues pertaining to the proposed sale and development of its environmentally impacted waterfront property, and he has represented a national energy company in its federal consistency review filing in Rhode Island under the Coastal Zone Management Act in connection with the proposed development of an LNG facility.

He has also represented purchasers in conducting due diligence for the acquisition of coastal properties and owners in the permitting and construction of new structures, or the substantial rehabilitation of existing structures, on coastal properties. His experience includes obtaining permits for sophisticated real estate acquisitions, leasing and development projects (including a major downtown Providence office building), complex Brownfields redevelopment projects, and winning the most significant real estate waterfront property rights case before the Rhode Island Supreme Court in over a century. In that case, he cleared title under the Public Trust

---

* The Rhode Island Supreme Court licenses all lawyers in the general practice of law. The Court does not license or certify any lawyer as an expert or specialist in any field of practice.

Doctrine to millions of dollars of waterfront properties built on filled tidal land. He also structured and negotiated the first major air rights development project in Providence, a hotel located in the air rights over a parking garage. Mr. Boehnert drafted the Design and Development Regulations for the seventy-seven acre Capital Center Special Development District abutting the State Capitol in Providence. Those regulations governed the use, design, and development of former rail yards and warehouses into a commercial, retail, and residential district, including the 1,400,000-square-foot Providence Place Mall, hundreds of residential units, and hundreds of thousands of square feet of office buildings.

Mr. Boehnert authored the first book to address the legal issues involving ocean zoning, entitled *Zoning the Oceans: The Next Big Step in Coastal Zone Management*, published by the American Bar Association in 2013. Mr. Boehnert has also published over one hundred articles and has addressed national conferences on international submerged lands, international coastal zone management, coastal permitting and coastal zone management, and land use law, as well as other professional groups on real estate and environmental law issues. He authored a chapter in a book on legal issues affecting the shopping center industry, and his article on the public trust doctrine was published in the *William and Mary Environmental Law and Policy Review*. He provides in-depth analysis of real estate, land use, and environmental law issues on his blog, www.rhodeislandpropertylaw.com, which is the only one of its kind in Rhode Island.

The Rhode Island Bar Association presented Mr. Boehnert with an award at its 2012 annual meeting for the most significant legal article published in the past year in the *Rhode Island Bar Journal*. The article addressed complex issues of federal and state's rights under the Coastal Zone Management Act's federal consistency program.

Mr. Boehnert is certified as a mediator and arbitrator and also provides consulting services for lawyers on sophisticated real estate and environmental projects.

He is listed in Best Lawyers in America and Super Lawyers, has held the highest rating in Martindale Hubbell for well over a decade (i.e., AV Preeminent), and was designated Best Lawyers Providence Real Estate Law Lawyer of the Year for 2014 and again for 2016.

Mr. Boehnert received his undergraduate degree summa cum laude from Boston University, attended the London School of Economics, and received his law degree cum laude from Georgetown University, where he served on the *Law and Policy in International Business Law Journal.*

He served as a congressional aide in both the US Senate and the US House of Representatives, and he clerked for Judge John H. Pratt in the Federal District Court for the District of Columbia.

Mr. Boehnert served two tours in the army infantry in Vietnam, where he was awarded the Purple Heart for wounds received in combat, two Bronze Stars, and the Vietnamese Cross of Gallantry, which was awarded by the then-government of the Republic of South Vietnam.

He lives on the waterfront in East Greenwich, Rhode Island.

INDEX